Runcie: On Reflection

Robert Alexander Kennedy Runcie, priest: born Birkenhead, Cheshire, 2 October 1921; MC, 1945; ordained deacon, 1950, priest, 1951; Curate, All Saints, Gosforth, 1950–2; Chaplain, Westcott House, Cambridge, 1953–4, Vice-Principal, 1954–6; Fellow, Dean and Assistant Tutor, Trinity Hall, Cambridge, 1956–60, Honorary Fellow, 1975; Vicar of Cuddesdon and Principal of Cuddesdon College, 1960–9; Bishop of St Albans, 1970–80; PC, 1980; Archbishop of Canterbury, 1980–91; Honorary Assistant Bishop of St Albans, 1991–2000; created 1991 Baron Runcie; married, 1957, Lindy Turner (one son, one daughter); died St Albans, Hertfordshire, 11 July 2000.[1]

Runcie

On Reflection

Compiled and edited by
Stephen Platten

CANTERBURY
PRESS
Norwich

First published in 2002 by the Canterbury Press Norwich
(a publishing imprint of Hymns Acient & Modern Limited,
a registered charity)
St Mary's Works, St Mary's Plain
Norwich, Norfolk NR3 3BH

www.scm-canterburypress.co.uk

British Library Cataloguing in Publication data

A catalogue record for this book is available
from the British Library

ISBN 1-85311-4707

Typeset by Rowland Phototypesetting Ltd,
Bury St Edmunds, Suffolk
and printed in Great Britain by
Creative Print and Design, Wales

Contents

Part Three: An Archbishop's Life

About the Contributors

Anthony Bryer is Emeritus Professor of Byzantine Studies at the University of Birmingham and an experienced lecturer on Swan Hellenic cruises

Andrew Brown is a freelance journalist who writes for the *Church Times* and was formerly religious affairs correspondent of the *Independent*

Richard Chartres is Bishop of London and was sometime Chaplain to the Archbishop of Canterbury

Richard Harries is Bishop of Oxford and a well-known broadcaster

Christopher Hill is Bishop of Stafford and was sometime Archbishop of Canterbury's Secretary for Ecumenical Affairs

Douglas Hurd is a former Foreign Secretary and Chairman of the Commission looking at the role of the Archbishop of Canterbury

Eric James is the retired director of Christian Action and was an adviser to the Archbishop of Canterbury's commission on urban priority areas

Graham James is Bishop of Norwich and was sometime Chaplain to the Archbishop of Canterbury

Stephen Platten is Dean of Norwich and was sometime Archbishop of Canterbury's Secretary for Ecumenical Affairs

David Say was Bishop of Rochester from 1961 to 1988

Mary Tanner was formerly Secretary to the Church of England Council for Christian Unity and Moderator of the World Council of Churches Faith and Order Commission

Desmond Tutu was formerly Archbishop of Cape Town and a renowned fighter against apartheid

Preface

Shortly after his memorial service in Westminster Abbey, a small group of friends and former staff members wondered whether it might be possible to put together a collection of essays on different aspects of Robert Runcie's achievement while Archbishop. This collection of reflections is not meant to be a full and critical life, although we hope that it will correct some misapprehensions and fill some lacunae left by what is widely felt to be the absence of an adequate biography. As a collection, then, this is neither intended to be a substitute biography nor the preparation of evidence for canonization. We realize that, as with all the most effective leaders, in the Church and elsewhere, it was Robert's flaws alongside his great talents that made him who he was and added to the richness of his character.

Robert Runcie had a highly developed sense of irony. A poignant sense of this overcame me as I realized that I was preparing this preface on the first anniversary of his death; it was a coincidence that he would have appreciated. On that very day I had been host to Klaus Kremkau, who with Robert and others had been one of the chief architects of the Meissen Agreement between the Church of England and the Evangelische Kirche von Deutschland. Klaus and I reflected upon all that Robert had given in this particular, fairly specialized, aspect of his ministry during his time as Archbishop of Canterbury. We reflected too on Robert's friendship, on his humour and on the joy that it had always given people to be in his company. It is these rather different strands that have come together to make this book.

We offer these remembrances and reflections in that spirit and, once again ironically, on the Feast of St Benedict; the anniversary of the day on which he died. Even in the final week of his life he had preached at the memorial service for Peter Moore, the former Dean of St Albans, an old friend and someone, to use Benedict's own words, who had been a fellow student with Robert in the 'school of the Lord's service'.

Stephen Platten
Norwich – 11 July 2001

Introduction
Runcie: Gownsman and Swordsman

STEPHEN PLATTEN

'I expect them all to be witty, stylishly self-ironic; both steeped in the classics and marinated in a very personal sense of the country's history and its place in the world.'[1] Although not describing archbishops in general or Robert Runcie in particular, it uncannily captures the man. In fact this is Peter Hennessy, in his *tour de force* on Prime Ministers, at this point focusing upon Harold Macmillan. The resonances in this description between Macmillan and Runcie are remarkable. A little later on Hennessy writes of Macmillan, his style and achievement: 'The whole effect was made possible partly by that constant tension within Macmillan between the "gownsman" and the "swordsman"; the scholar and the warrior . . .' Macmillan himself had coined this juxtaposition in an aside in his diary in 1954 on officialdom and notably officialdom in the treasury. He had written there:

> They were all "gownsmen" – none 'sword and cloak men'. They are against the aristocracy; the successful businessman; and the adventurer (in its widest sense). They are like the clergy in the pre-Reformation times. It was against them, rather than against theological doctrine, that our ancestors revolted.[2]

Now we need not take Macmillan's invective too seriously to see some of the parallels. Admittedly Robert Runcie did not come with the same pedigree – upper middle class and married into the aristocracy – but many of the other parallels are clear. Both were at least partially of Scottish descent: Robert's father was from Greenock in Scotland. Both had distinguished wartime military careers – Macmillan being wounded with a shattered pelvis at the Somme, Robert being awarded an MC for conspicuous bravery for rescuing a soldier from a burning tank. Both had read 'Greats' at Oxford and had distinguished themselves in their studies. Both had a very clear historical consciousness and a most engaging, self-mocking humour coupled with a gift for self-confident understatement. One cannot press the analogy too far, but Runcie remained a gownsman throughout his life. Like Macmillan, his style was patrician. He was admired by almost all his episcopal colleagues, but his presence, bearing, sharpness of judgement and discernment meant that on occasion they were not a little intimidated by him. He was not a natural committee man, though never shrank from committee work. When chairing the House of Bishops, for example, it was sometimes what he did *not* say that could be withering. But those who served with him knew his unique capacity for friendship and even those who felt withered rarely felt alienated.

The background to Robert's emergence as archbishop is itself illuminating. In the immediate post-war years, Geoffrey Fisher did a remarkable job in sorting out both the administration and canon law of the Church of England. The extent of his achievement is often overshadowed by his personality which remained that of an Edwardian public school headmaster long after he relinquished his role as Headmaster of Repton. It was a style which would have been unthinkable even 10 years after he retired. The bridge between Fisher's archiepiscopal headmastership and a more contemporary model was provided, ironically, through one of his pupils at Repton – Michael Ramsey. Ramsey was a completely different character, so different that Owen Chadwick in his biography of Ramsey recalls Fisher's blandishments to Harold Macmillan in his attempt to stop Ramsey's appointment. Macmillan said to Ramsey: 'Fisher doesn't seem to approve of you.' Ramsey defended him: 'Fisher', he said, 'was my headmaster and has known all my deficiencies for a long time.' 'Well,' said Macmillan, 'he is not going to be my headmaster.'[3] Fisher may not have been too far off the mark in his criticisms when he noted Ramsey's penchant for theologizing at York at the expense of direct leadership and administration. Ramsey's intellectual ability, his political liberalism and the image he projected – in the words of some journalists, like a 'woolly prophet' – did certainly effect a transition into a different world. On occasion he would courageously engage with political issues, as with Ian Smith's Rhodesian UDI for example. Nevertheless his lack of interest in synods and committees may have allowed both the Church of England and the Anglican Communion to drift into building bureaucracies which would reap a dubious harvest. Robert Runcie would later find himself one of the doubtful beneficiaries of Ramsey's other-worldly approach. With Donald Coggan, the Church of England gained an archbishop who in some ways was less in tune with the times than his predecessor. Coggan, a biblical scholar and a moderate evangelical of great dignity and integrity, reflected an ethos within society that had largely disappeared; he radiated a certain naivety. In 1975 his Call to the Nation not only fell on deaf ears but misjudged the spirit of the age – it was tinged with a bygone moralism. Retired Regius Professor of Moral Theology at Christ Church, Oxford, Vigo Demant, commented gnomically upon the initiative: 'Same old thing, the world would be so much better if only it were so much better!'[4]

It was into this void that Robert Runcie would be catapulted in the 1980s. A measure of changing times was that this was the first occasion when newspapers ran a sort of pre-election profiling of possible candidates. Photographs of candidates, some more credible than others, appeared, even in the broadsheet newspapers; this speculation fell only just short of placing 'bookies' odds' next to the pictures. The Crown Appointments' Commission was chaired by Sir Richard O'Brien, a radically minded businessman who ran the government's Manpower Services Commission and who would later chair Faith in the City, the Archbishop of Canterbury's Commission on Urban Priority Areas which would be commissioned by Robert Runcie. The story is told that when Margaret Thatcher wrote to Runcie asking if she might put his name to the Queen nominating him as the next Archbishop of Canterbury, he took six weeks to answer, necessitating the 'Iron Lady' to telephone him and to encourage him to make up his mind. Accepting this nomination, he embarked upon his new work striking an image as the first modern Archbishop of Canterbury, representing an entirely new style of archiepiscopate. One symbolic indication of this was his appearance on the Michael Parkinson show. For all Robert's classical education and historical consciousness, he was also a thoroughly contemporary archbishop. His grasp of the ambiguities of human nature combined with an extraordinary intelligence in his dealings with people gave him formidable qualities for the role that had been handed on to him. He was acutely aware of the significance of this role and it was this that led to an insistence on perfectionism in both substance and style that could be more than demanding upon both staff and the wider 'court' which grew around him. Subtlety and an appreciation of the different sides to any argument contributed to that perception shared by many that he had 'nailed his colours to the fence' and this did not make decision-making easier.

His classical but Christian humanist education emphasized for him the fundamental mystery at the heart of all human beings. This led to a multiplication of points of view and to a variety of arguments in the face of seemingly intractable problems. He knew that people at times saw him as agonized, indecisive and tortuous but in his heart he believed this complexity to be unavoidable. The official portrait at Lambeth by David Poole captures the mixture of humour and agonized uncertainty in the man with great sensitivity.

Robert's acute appreciation of the mystery of human nature expressed itself both in his contribution to public political life and in the manner in which he undertook the impossible task of being Archbishop of Canterbury. As later chapters will reveal in more detail, Robert engaged in public affairs with a remarkable mixture of subtlety and courage. This needs to be placed alongside the crude journalistic reports of clashes with the government and notably with Mrs Thatcher. He had known Margaret Thatcher when they were both undergraduates at Oxford, after the Second World War. Interestingly enough, Robert had been a member of the Oxford University Conservative Association of which Margaret Roberts, as she then was, was President; characteristically he combined this with membership of the Labour Club! Lady Thatcher claimed not to remember Robert from her Oxford days and this may well reflect fairly accurately their very different views of human life – Runcie was ever an acute observer of human beings; Margaret Thatcher was much more attached to a particular view of life. Certainly, they were hardly like personalities, but Robert had more admiration for her courage and sense of purpose than some would give credit for in the press coverage at the time. It was in style that they were at such variance and also in their appreciation of the frailties of human nature. Robert could see that such frailty meant that any policy based upon the 'survival of the fittest' was bound to mean the crushing of those least equipped to cope, either through lack of intellectual strength or insufficient emotional stamina. He saw the pragmatic sense of some of the Thatcher policies and of 'firm government' but he was equally aware of the casualties of change. The riots down the road from Lambeth, in Brixton, or in Toxteth – in the city of his birth – were vivid reminders of this. It was such perceptions that encouraged him to commission the report that would eventually be titled *Faith in the City*. Arguably this was one of the most influential reports on English society ever commissioned by the Christian Church; undoubtedly Michael Heseltine's initiatives to renew inner-city suburbs were stimulated and prompted by this report. The same could be said of more recent attempts to regenerate our inner cities. Anthony Howard wrote recently in *The Times*:

However tough they may have appeared at the time, the Thatcher years were perversely rather helpful ones for the Church of England. It was the gloomy Dean of St Pauls, W. R. Inge, who once famously observed that any church which enters into marriage with the spirit of the age 'will soon find itself a widow in the next'. On that ground alone it will always redound greatly to Robert Runcie's credit that he resisted the obvious temptation to endorse or underwrite the Thatcher revolution even at the height of its success.

Instead, along with John Habgood (his archiepiscopal colleague at York), he saw to it that for 11 long years the Church provided just about the most effective critique of the whole Thatcherite ethos. That may not have made life easy either at Lambeth Palace or at Bishopthorpe, but at least between them the two archbishops ensured that the Church always possessed a voice in the national debate – and one that sometimes (as over its 1985 report *Faith in the City*) carried a considerable resonance.[5]

That quotation is all the more compelling coming from a political commentator rather than from a professional churchman
or moral theologian. At a consultation at St George's House,
Windsor, in the 1980s, the then Trade Union Fellow (at that
time a regular slot at Windsor) reflected: 'You keep it up,' (by
you he meant the Church), 'you are the only opposition the
country has; we in the Labour party seem to have given up!'

When Robert Runcie began his work as Archbishop, he would
have been startled had someone suggested that in five years he
would effectively be leading the opposition in the absence of
any real political alternative. But how did Robert's approach
work itself out in terms of general strategy in relation to the
task of being Archbishop? To begin with he saw that the role
had some parallels with that of a cabinet minister or even that
of a leader of government. This required an adequate, professionally equipped staff since he could not be expected to be
an expert or polymath in the extraordinary range of matters
upon which an archbishop would be called to comment. It
would be misleading to suggest that Robert Runcie 'invented'
the notion of a Lambeth staff. The role of chaplain, for example,
extended back a long way. Randall Davidson, for example, had
been chaplain to Archbishop Tait; it was this that, very early
on in his ministry, had brought him to the attention of Queen
Victoria and which had led him to being appointed to the Deanery of Windsor in his early thirties. George Bell too had cut his
teeth in fulfilling the role of chaplain during the early part of
the twentieth century when he had worked for Randall Davidson. The role of chaplain developed into a mirror image of the
classical pattern of the personal private secretary.

During Robert's time the role developed still further, such that
the chaplain became, in Shakespearian phrase, 'a snapper-up of
unconsidered trifles'. It was this aspect of the role that led
eventually to the chaplain taking into his remit the responsibility
for advice and support to the archbishop in his increasing work
with inter-faith issues. The chaplain, then, was the ultimate gen-
eralist among the archbishop's staff and the key confidant and
friend in all that he was called to do. The ecumenical support
staff had its beginnings in 1933 with the appointment of John
Douglas as the Honorary Secretary of the newly formed Council

for Foreign Relations. During Michael Ramsey's archiepiscopate Robert Beloe had been lay staff officer dealing with some political and establishment matters and Geoffrey Tiarks as Bishop of Maidstone had been senior chaplain, a sort of chief staff officer.

What Robert began to establish was a more comprehensive staffing, reaching across different areas. Eve Keatley, bringing a wealth of professional experience from the BBC, was appointed as the first press officer at Lambeth. Previously this role had been carried out jointly for the General Synod and the Archbishop of Canterbury across the river in Church House. Tensions, however, had grown in this relationship – tensions which Robert had identified. It was not the first time that there had needed to be both closeness and distance between Lambeth and its neighbours across the Thames. Archbishop Baldwin, in the late twelfth century, had seen the strategic sense in establishing a residence in the capital. He located it across the river from the royal palace in Westminster – close enough for swift communication but suitably detached to retain independence. Robert Runcie saw that a similar principle applied in the modern day. Church House was the headquarters of the central councils of the church to which he as Archbishop was firmly committed; Lambeth Palace, however, was the residence of the Archbishop's household. Robert knew that the Archbishop of Canterbury was not just the leader of the Church of England and its councils, but also the key religious statesmen, speaking for the country as a whole in its religious and spiritual aspects. Eve Keatley's new post captured this perception very clearly; and she was the first staff appointment to be funded initially by the Lambeth Fund, which had been brought into being through the work of Hector Laing. Later on the Lambeth Press Officer would become a charge on central church funds through the Church Commissioners.

The creation of a secretariat for Anglican Communion affairs was entirely the initiative of the new Archbishop; he had seen the need for this even during his time as Bishop of St Albans. The choice of Terry Waite was inspired, although he was soon to be drawn away from his essential role as increasingly he became enmeshed in the hostage rescue initiatives. Robert admired Terry's personal gifts and his flair; at a rather dull reception at Lambeth, during the hostage crisis, Robert remarked to a colleague: 'If Terry had been here, we'd have had a steel band!' Nevertheless Robert was also aware that Terry was a free spirit who later became engulfed in the wider American intelligence intrigue surrounding the Oliver North affair. Following Terry Waite's captivity, Roger Symon systematically built up an expertise in Anglican Communion affairs and consolidated the work of the Archbishop in this area. Then the Council for Foreign Relations was transformed into a secretariat of ecumenical affairs under the leadership of Canon Christopher Hill. Here in the realm of ecumenical affairs, the separate household of the Archbishop was of paramount importance. Among the ancient churches, the Archbishop of Canterbury was identified effectively as a 'Patriarch' and thus needed the diplomatic advice and support offered by ecumenical specialists. Finally, the lay staff officer role was enhanced and transformed under Robert's leadership. In this role, Robert had inherited Michael Kinchin-Smith from Donald Coggan. Kinchin-Smith had moved to Lambeth from a senior post in the BBC and he was succeeded by Wilfred Grenville-Grey. Both of these brought with them the strengths of a senior lay churchman. With the appointment of John Lyttle, now styled as Secretary for Public Affairs, came someone who knew the political establishment from the inside; he had been on the political staff of both Roy Jenkins and Shirley Williams. His role now covered the political, ethical and establishment spheres and his previous political experience combined with his time as secretary to the Police Complaints Authority brought a particular professionalism, even though Lyttle would have to spend much of his time on the hostage issue. Robert also re-established a senior staff role in the form of a 'Chief of Staff' who eventually became known as Bishop at Lambeth. This was a skilful move. By placing a former diocesan bishop in that role he had a right-hand man who both had appropriate experience and who would naturally be taken seriously by other diocesan bishops. The Bishop at Lambeth was not (and was never intended to be) involved directly in the Archbishop's ministry, accompanying him on visits or numerous church services; this remained the territory of the chaplain and the specialist staff members. The Bishop at Lambeth would deal with senior personnel issues, clergy discipline, and consultation between the Archbishop, General Synod officers and the dioceses. Together with a first-rate personal secretary and with a cohort of younger (often graduate) secretaries the Lambeth staff was a group to be taken seriously. The experience, expertise and intelligence brought together under the direction of a senior episcopal colleague lent great strength to the Archbishop's private office.

Robert never allowed what was still a relatively modest staff to become an introverted 'kitchen cabinet'. Instead, the kaleidoscopic network of friends that he had built up throughout his life formed an extraordinary matrix of people upon whom he could call to obtain the very best briefing on whatever subject he might be required to comment upon. There were, for example, the Scots Guards friendships: Willie Whitelaw, Chips Maclean and Hector Laing could offer advice, contacts or assistance in the realms of politics, the establishment, the military or business, and they did! Sir Charles (Chips) Maclean had been Lord Chamberlain. Hector Laing helped put the Lambeth operation on a sound financial footing and it would be Willie Whitelaw who would speak at an amazing farewell party for the retiring Archbishop in 1991. With suitable irony, the party took place at the Banqueting Hall in Whitehall, the very place from which Charles I had stepped out on to the scaffold on that very day, 30 January, 342 years earlier! All grist to the Runcie style mill with its familiar self-mocking twist in his speech to colleagues and friends.

Then there were the Trinity Hall contacts including Launcelot Fleming who had married Robert and Lindy; academics like Graham Howes, the sociologist, and others who would provide briefing on countless specialist topics. Similarly Oxford and Brasenose came to the Archbishop's assistance; Robert would also use his Oxford experience to good effect in his role as Visitor to All Souls. Westcott House, where he was trained for the priesthood and later returned as Vice-Principal, had been equally fertile soil. Bill Vanstone, one of the most able priests of his generation, remained a lifelong friend and a fecund source for theological stimulation where sermons and speech preparation required such material. In the post-war years Westcott had produced a remarkable battalion of able clergy who would dominate the bench of bishops in the late 1960s and for much of the 1970s and 1980s. John Habgood had followed Robert as Vice-Principal there. Patrick Rodger, later Bishop of Manchester and then Oxford and a great ecumenist, had been a contemporary of Robert's. Cuddesdon, where Robert was Principal from 1960 to 1970 had yielded rich friendships and contacts which Robert never let go. He loved being vicar of the village and he cherished the friendships he made there well into his retirement. But it was not only these friendships and contacts close to home. If as a member of staff one entered Lambeth Palace even as late as 11 o'clock at night – and that was quite likely for Robert was a taskmaster both for others and for himself – as you climbed the stairs you would hear Robert's unmistakable tones on the telephone. It might be a friend on the east coast of the USA, a bishop in Australia, Desmond Tutu from Cape Town or an Orthodox from eastern Europe. There would be bursts of mirth from Robert's end of the telephone line but much seriousness too as he strove to keep together the 'rebellious house' that is the Anglican Communion, in his own inimitable personal style. This capacity for nurturing and cherishing profound friendships lay close to the heart of both Robert's style and his effectiveness as Archbishop. The manner in which Robert prepared both for visits and for speeches and sermons relates directly to this capacity for friendship.

Even this capacity for friendship, however, could be dangerous. A famous example relates to the case of the *Crockford's* preface controversy. Gary Bennett, Fellow (and formerly Dean) of New College, Oxford, and an accomplished ecclesiastical historian, frequently drafted material for Robert. As the years passed, so Bennett saw friends and colleagues gaining preferment in the Church of England. He seems to have believed that his work for the Archbishop should eventually have resulted in some sort of reward. The Archbishop of Canterbury has, however, little power over patronage. Bennett, for whatever reason, received no preferment and so, when asked to be the author of the anonymous preface to the 1987 edition of *Crockford's Clerical Directory*, used this opportunity to express some of his bitterness about the Church of England establishment and particularly in relation to the Archbishop's part within it. The newspapers tracked down the authorship of the preface and when this became known, Bennett took his own life. The whole catalogue of circumstances understandably left a bitter aftertaste. One of Robert Runcie's collaborators and confidants had turned on his friend and ultimately the episode had led to his premature and tragic death. This was a dark irony for Robert, a man for whom friendship was one of the most marked characteristics of his life.

Humphrey Carpenter's controversial biography focused critically on the manner in which Robert put together his key speeches, lectures and sermons as Archbishop and it is important to give some space to this issue here. Perhaps one should begin by emphasizing the consciousness that Robert had of his role and of the office of Archbishop of Canterbury. He was clear that when he spoke he spoke not as Robert Runcie, a private citizen, or even an individual clergyman. Instead, he spoke as the present occupant of a key office with something of a corporate responsibility about it – when he spoke it was for the Church of England, for the Anglican Communion and for the Christian faith itself. His conviction that this was a corporate role required research, writing and preparation from others, both his personal staff and his great multitude of friends. His approach to speaking and writing was not some form of escape from this crucial role; instead it was a key affirmation of the essential nature of his task as Archbishop and its significance in the world of the wider Church. A couple of examples press this point home.

In early 1990 there was a great gathering in Westminster Cathedral to celebrate the twenty-fifth anniversary of the Decree on Ecumenism of the Second Vatican Council which had done so much to encourage the movement towards Christian unity. There were to be no less than three homilies, but Robert's was to be the set piece. As usual the staff were put to work early on to gather material and to produce some basic drafts for the Archbishop's use. How should one begin? Who could provide suitable research? A number of names were reeled off by the Archbishop, including some well-known ecumenists – Oliver Tomkins was a key source, but people from other churches, including notably a Roman Catholic priest who had been on

Robert's staff at Cuddesdon – all were pressed into service. A week or so later and the material needed to be edited and processed. Not only did his staff receive material from the people whose names he had reeled off at the beginning, far more came thudding on to the mat behind the Lambeth letter box! Robert had in the days following the initial briefing encountered friends in the corridors of Church House and at a number of other gatherings that he had attended. Each time he had mentioned the address which he had to give and had casually asked for more briefing.

The process that followed was not always easy. If someone sent in briefing material they would be keen for it to be used in some way or another. An intricately woven text which might form the foundation of the Archbishop's address would be put together and sent over for his scrutiny. If you felt that here were the foundations of a decent piece of work, you also knew it had its weaknesses. A few days later, when you were called into the Archbishop's study, you would go through the work with him with infinite care and you would hope that the lacunae might not stare out at him too clearly. If the material was good he would be grateful and use it but the weaknesses never passed him by. 'What does this mean in this paragraph here – this needs more work!' He was ever the don, ever the 'gownsman'.

But his capacity for friendship and for understanding people bubbled over into this process too. In some of the chapters which follow, other writers refer to Robert's art of understatement and his tendency towards self-mockery. One particular example comes to mind. As a staff we were preparing the Archbishop for the final meeting of the British Council of Churches at Swanwick in Derbyshire. It was a poignant occasion for many of the long-serving warriors in the ecumenical battlefield. The organization which they had fought to establish was to extinguish itself in an act of voluntary suicide. It was to be both a funeral wake and a christening party for the new organizations which had just been born. Robert was the key figure at this event. He knew the people well and his enduring capacity for friendship meant that he could help transform this wake into a celebration as the churches looked to the new instruments of unity. At the heart of all this would lie an address he was to give, outlining and commending to all present the five new organizations, four of them confined to the individual countries which make up Britain and Ireland. How should he begin this address and somehow strike the right note with a lightness of touch and yet a relevance to the process that was about to be launched?

There was a myth often repeated at Lambeth about Robert addressing the Headmasters' Conference held, rather unusually on this occasion, in Aberdeen. He is purported to have begun: 'It is a very long time since I was last in this part of England.' Doubtless if it did happen it was a slip of the tongue, but the story goes that a notable silence followed. This is most likely remembering the amount of Scots' *amour propre* that is likely to have been around, and remembering Robert's own Scottish ancestry. This story was served up as a possible starter for his BCC Swanwick address. His response was immediate and sharp: 'I never said that!' 'People have said you did, Archbishop,' the staff member meekly replied. 'I'm sure that I could never have said that,' he repeated, but as he did so that well-known quizzical, agonized expression crept across his face. 'Well, even if I didn't say it, it's a good story – it contains its own humour and it's about nationality.' Duly it took its place as the starting point for his address. Here, as elsewhere, the process was painstaking. Knowing the significance of the office that had been handed to him, Robert Runcie was forced to be a perfectionist. Draft after draft was produced and even in the car on the way to the event he would be fiddling with phrases and still polishing it up as he made his way up the steps to deliver it.

During his time as Archbishop and since, much energy and ink have been expended in attempts to decide what the final effects of his mode of operating were. Was he not simply a mouthpiece for the views of others? Did his own views, personality or outlook on the world ever emerge in the countless addresses, lectures, sermons and speeches that he gave? Had he not become like the figure at the helm of government simply spouting the policy of a bureaucracy? Did he not have the courage of his convictions? Such a conclusion would be miles from the truth. His dependence upon briefing and speech writers is undeniable. He knew that he could not possibly deliver material of the quality required over such a vast range without a whole army of people giving of their best. Part of Robert's intelligence, however, was to go back one or more stages beyond the process of drafting and gleaning material. He realized that to be effective he needed to gather to himself, both on his personal staff and among his wider circle of friends, people who understood not only his style (although that was crucial) but also something of the context and background from which his own theology had issued. After all it was not Robert Runcie who people had come to hear, but the Archbishop of Canterbury. Now this network of friendships falls further into place. His role was to focus through the office the essence of Christian truth for his age. Some people have referred to Robert as the last Renaissance humanist Archbishop of Canterbury. It is impossible and even irrelevant to assess the truth of that claim, but undoubtedly it is from that world and that consciousness that Robert's own reflections, feelings and beliefs emerged.

When looking back at his writings, it is perhaps best to follow the principles that contemporary critics apply to the New Testament documents. The method known as redaction criticism presupposes that the Gospel writers were creative editors. They took over material, moulded it, added their own contribution and finally polished it and fashioned it for publication. If such a process did take place it is difficult if not impossible to know when a particular saying goes back to Jesus himself or whether it comes from another source available to the evangelist, or from the evangelist's own pen. What is clear in the case of the evangelists is that within each Gospel there is a consistency of style which we now describe as Lucan, Markan, Johannine or Matthean. This might be the best model to apply to Robert's addresses, sermons and lectures. There is no doubting the overall consistency of the Runcie style or that whenever content or style jarred, the material would be rewritten again and again and tinkered with to the last moment. For all his dependence on briefing, Robert was never the mouthpiece of a bureaucracy or the purveyor of tired language or second-hand thoughts. His own humanity and intelligence were more than sufficient to safeguard against these dangers.

In these reflections there is much emphasis not only on

Robert's capacity for friendship but also on his humour. It would be a mistake to suggest that this element of his personality was flip, superficial or glib. Robert's humour issued from the richness and intelligence of his humanity. Reference was made earlier to the official portrait of Robert at Lambeth by David Poole, a portrait that captures perfectly both Robert's humour and the agony and anxiety that lay at the heart of his character. Decisions were never easy for him and the pressures of his role as Archbishop made this more difficult still. His personal staff were said to have a further responsibility of helping to soak up his anxiety. The pressures and expectations placed upon Archbishops of Canterbury are both unrealistic and unreasonable. It is hard to imagine anyone who would not be pressed into an anxious frame of mind through the impossible requirements of the job. But in Robert it was more than simply the insecurities fuelled by the demands of the role. Some of the most telling photographs of him portray an agony of mind which reflected a real appreciation of the human condition and its ambiguities. This is where his experiences as a swordsman came to the surface.

There is a current expression which describes people as having had a 'good war'. That could certainly be said of Robert Runcie. When preaching in the cathedral at Portsmouth in 1984, at a service to dedicate a window in memory of D-Day, Robert recalled rolling his tank 'down the flats' at Gosport in training for the real thing. His courage in the war was rewarded with a Military Cross. Some of the most poignant reflections on his wartime experience emerged in a television documentary produced by James, his son, only a week before Robert died. The programme has been acknowledged as something of a masterpiece. James asked him about his feelings when he, with his regiment, entered and liberated the concentration camp at Belsen. Robert talked of the stench and the pall over the place and James asked whether his father 'had seen the heart of darkness'. Robert commented: 'A war which shut down Belsen was a war worth fighting; you felt you had touched evil.'[6]

The Second World War revealed his more agonized side. He remembered the military training that told him he must hate the enemy, but he could not imagine hating a German. After one particular tank battle he and some fellow soldiers went over to examine a burnt out German tank. Five German soldiers lay dead and Robert could think only of sweethearts and mothers whose lives would be shattered. It was this sort of experience that lent a manifest authenticity to the Falklands' sermon.

This final television interview also focused on his particular religious sense. He appreciated it when someone said of him, 'There's quite a lot of you that isn't a clergyman.' There was no obvious piety to him and some accused him of cynicism in relation to prayer and the Church. Yet there was an unquestioned seriousness about him in spite of all the humour. Three times in the interview he referred to something outside himself influencing the sort of person he was going to be. He remarked on this as he remembered the onset of his father's blindness. Then later on he spoke of 'a good which will come from outside yourselves'. Finally, he reflected that: 'Most of the worthwhile things in life came from outside myself rather than from my own ambition.' He admitted that as an individual he was always quite guarded, but noted also: 'I didn't try to cultivate an air of mystery – but there is undeniably a fundamental mystery to human beings.'

These essays aim to look at different aspects of Robert Runcie, the man, the archbishop, the friend. In different ways they pick up some of the ambiguities that have begun to emerge in this brief introduction. Swordsman and gownsman combined in Robert Runcie but the deepest foundations of all this lay in a man of extraordinarily rich humanity. He had been fashioned through the Christian humanistic influences of the English educational system and perhaps most notably the culturally conservative but open traditions of the Oxford 'Greats' school.

Robert confessed an incarnational faith, and was a living example of incarnational truth. It was unquestionably his rich humanity that offered in subtle and sophisticated ways signposts to God. It was these very same traits and attributes which made him a scandal to those who disliked him but for those who worked with him, alongside his humour and his compassion, there was always more to discover of his commitment to the crucial role that had been handed on to him. He used all the intelligence and experiences of a rich and varied life and brought them to bear on the task in hand. When asked by his son what he had learned from cancer, he replied: 'It has given me time to harvest life.' Some glimpses of that harvest follow in this book.

Bishop, Companion and Friend: Runcie Remembered

GRAHAM JAMES

*The address given at Robert Runcie's funeral, 22 July 2000
in St Alban's Cathedral*

To begin with two texts is a very un-Runcie-like practice. The first is from Luke's Gospel:

> all who exalt themselves will be humbled, but all who humble themselves will be exalted. (Luke 18.14)

The second comes from St Paul, writing to the Corinthians:

> I have become all things to all people, so that I might by any means save some. I do it all for the sake of the gospel. (1 Cor. 9.22–23)

It is odd that this missionary virtue should be looked upon with suspicion in our own day. St Paul became all things to all people through conviction, not uncertainty. He says, 'To the weak I became weak so that I might win the weak ... To the Jews I became a Jew in order to win Jews'. It didn't always work, of course. When Paul preached in the Areopagus he tried eloquence to impress the sophisticated Athenians. But he founded no church there. Yet to the Corinthians Paul spoke of the Church as the Body of Christ in a city where the human body was the source of peaks of sensual excitement. These days we might say that Paul began where people were to draw them to faith in Jesus Christ. Paul's subtlety has often been underappreciated – but then subtlety, if true to itself, should pass unnoticed.

In many respects Robert Runcie was not at all like St Paul. Height, for example. According to Paul's account of himself he was neither attractive, tall nor elegant. Sometimes people were surprised to discover that Robert Runcie had such a fine bearing. On the way out of Liverpool Cathedral one day a woman greeted him with: 'Well, fancy that. I thought you were a little shrimp of a man.'

Robert loved returning to honest Merseyside and to St Faith's, Great Crosby, where the colour, order and beauty of the Catholic tradition of the Church of England had captured his soul as a young man. He received his religion through the eyes quite as much as through the ears. His faith was a faith of all the senses. Sermons were to be elegant, poetic, an art form. They were laboured over, words weighed for both truth and impact. They were to reflect the attractiveness of God. Robert wanted people to be drawn in their humanity to the God in whose image they were made. He always saw God in them as well as the flaws and failures that make human beings seem so frequently ridiculous. It is this incongruity between our status as children of God and our vanity and foolishness that was the source of so much of his humour. That was why he was so patient with a fallen world and a defective Church. He could never be a recruit for the single issue fanatic or the moralizing majority. His sense of proportion frequently irritated them.

But this did not eradicate Robert's urge to identify with whoever he met. To the Jews he became a Jew. With the weak he was weak. He would connect. 'When I was a country vicar in Oxfordshire', he would say to the rural clergy, rather than 'when I was a theological college principal', which took up a shade more of his time at Cuddesdon. 'When I was a curate on Tyneside' was a good line for the inner city, though some of the leafy boulevards of Gosforth do stretch the boundaries of inner-city ministry a bit. I heard him describe his father variously as 'an agnostic Presbyterian' or 'a Presbyterian agnostic', depending on just what degree of subtlety was appropriate. His mother was frequently mentioned with affection as 'a hairdresser on an ocean-going liner'. In all this there was a deep love for his roots, his history and his family. He instinctively put himself at the service of others. That was why he was a good pastor. His was an incarnate religion.

In many ways the episcopate is not family friendly. The

diocese – let alone a worldwide Communion – is an irritating competitor for the wife seeking her husband's attention or the child or teenager wanting some fatherly care. The freshness and liveliness of the Runcie family shows how it can be done, but Robert would never have been able to tell you how. That's partly the secret. Before we had ever met Lindy, my wife had an article written by Lindy on display in our kitchen. It was titled, 'Clergy Wives Are People Too'. There has never been any doubt about that in Lindy's case. With her by his side there was no chance of Robert becoming donnish and remote.

Robert Runcie was an achiever but curiously resistant to recalling his achievements. I cannot remember a single occasion when he made reference himself to his Military Cross, his first in Greats or to other activities that could have made him a bore rather than a boon companion. Robert was reticent. That's one of the reasons why so many of us loved him.

He was also curiously detached from material possessions. This wasn't because he lacked an aesthetic eye. He loved beautiful things, but there was a spareness to him and a discipline as well. He may have liked fine wines, but his intake was moderate, which is perhaps why he needed a succession of chaplains who could be relied upon to finish any bottle of champagne.

Those few of us privileged to work with Robert Runcie also prayed with him every day. He was incapable of public displays of piety, but his Christianity permeated the whole of his personality. It was no easy faith. There was nothing glib about it. That was why it convinced, or, put better, he convinced. There is, of course, a much bigger tale to be told. There is the story of the tank commander; the trainer of clergy; the Bishop of St Albans who made this diocese an exciting place and who loved this city; the priest whose instinct it was to identify with institutions yet who became the focus in the eighties for dissent from prevailing political orthodoxy; the Archbishop who travelled the Anglican Communion supporting those in more threatening situations to which Desmond Tutu's presence today is testimony; the ecumenist – who will ever forget the Papal visit, though the real breakthrough of his time came with the Lutheran and Reformed churches in Germany. Then there was the retired Archbishop whose ministry continued to the very last. Only days before his own death he delivered his final address for Peter Moore's funeral. The day before on the telephone he tried out a few sentences on me. Dying himself, he wanted to get exactly right what he said to honour a friend and colleague and to honour God. He spent himself.

There is more to be said, but we honour Robert Runcie the man, the husband, the father and grandfather, the companion and friend, the Christian priest and bishop. He left people feeling better – more in touch with themselves and with God – for having met and known him. He was Good News, and that is spiritual stature.

A poem by Ann Lewin called 'After Word' draws together our remembrances of Robert.

> Thus heavens and earth were
> Finished, and were good. But
> In the middle of the night, God woke.
> 'It might be burdensome,' he thought,
> 'To give dominion over all created things
> To earthling folk; lest they should
> Take themselves too seriously,
> I'll give them music and a
> Sense of fun, to lighten duty and
> Enliven praise.'
> So in wise mercy did Creator God.
> And all the seventh day, he rested,
> Well content.[1]

We delight in Robert Runcie's life and ministry which has lightened duty and enlivened praise. Robert, may you now rest in the refreshing peace of our Creator God, to whose wise mercy we commit you, well content. Well content. Amen.

PART ONE

An Archbishop's Lot

1. Reluctant Crusader: Runcie and the State

DOUGLAS HURD

To glance through the press cuttings on Robert Runcie's relationship with the Conservative Government of the 1980s is to revisit a battlefield of apparent conflict, even carnage. The Archbishop was represented in turn as an appeaser of Argentine aggression, a purveyor of Marxist theology, and an impotent leader of a church reluctant to bring traditional morality into the fight against the moral decay of our society. More particularly, Robert Runcie was portrayed as locked in mortal combat with a dynamic Prime Minister – indeed at one stage he was described as the only effective opposition, given the decline of the main Opposition party during much of his term of office. Most of this is nonsense, and illustrates the decay of the modern British press, rather than of the established Church and its leader.

In terms of his personality Robert Runcie was a genial member of the establishment with a small 'e'. It was impossible to dislike him, and Margaret Thatcher made no attempt to do so. It sounds frivolous, but my most persistent memory of the Archbishop is of an elegant, amiable figure in a purple vest, standing in one of the galleries at Buckingham Palace, waiting for the start of a State Banquet for some foreign head of state. Whether as Home Secretary or Foreign Secretary, I would be greeted congenially by this urbane figure, entirely at home in his surroundings, who would then move behind a pillar into light-hearted conversation which, however, was never irrelevant to his job or mine. Because Robert Runcie was a reluctant crusader, he was an effective one, a paradox difficult to explain except in a strictly English context. The famous sermon in St Paul's Cathedral at the Memorial Service after the Falklands War is a case in point. Not every Archbishop can win a Military Cross, but the fact that this Archbishop had done so must have been in the minds of everybody at that service. An Archbishop who has led troops in battle will be listened to with particular attention on matters of peace and war. Most people rereading Robert Runcie's Falklands sermon now would find it hard to understand the commotion which it caused. He made it clear that he supported the need for the British expedition to retake the Falklands. If he had gone on from that simply to preach a sermon which rejoiced in victory and said nothing about the evils of war, if he had failed to mention the need to pray for the bereaved Argentinian families, this would have been a crude perversion of Christian thought. The harm done by such an alternative sermon would have been felt by the Church, and indeed by Britain, for years to come. It would have set a disastrous example.

Robert Runcie, however, engaged with social issues more broadly and, more important in the relationship between Church and Government, with the Church's study *Faith in the City*. One of my colleagues, snatching at a headline, absurdly described the report at the time as Marxist theology. There was a school of thought at the far edge of Thatcherism which did indeed regard the creation of wealth as a moral good in itself, and played down any talk of social responsibility as likely to clog up the market processes from which everyone would eventually benefit. The Prime Minister herself went quite far in this direction, for example, in her speech to the General Assembly of the Church of Scotland, but usually her policies were more comprehending and practical than her rhetoric. *Faith in the City*, well before it was fashionable to do so, analysed the main social problem of our country, namely, the formation of a separate underclass on the outskirts and in the centre of many of our large cities.[1] This section of society is held down not by the Government nor by the police, but by poverty, crime and hopelessness. In some moods Mrs Thatcher's Government accepted this analysis, as its policies on the inner cities and its successive initiatives, for example, Michael Heseltine's care of Merseyside, showed. The valid criticism of *Faith in the City* was not directed at its analysis, but at one part of its solutions. *Faith in the City* over-stated the likely effectiveness of bureaucratic intervention. At the time of writing we have a Government which has far more public money at its disposal than any of its recent predecessors of any party, and is in danger of falling into the same illusion. Schemes on this basis require accountability, and accountability involves bureaucracy. Whether one looks at the National Health Service, our schools and universities, or our police, we see what has been christened the audit society, that is, a world of many worthwhile but confused and overlapping endeavours, often frustrated by the infinite setting of targets and drafting of assessments.

That is why the most valuable part of *Faith in the City*, after its compelling analysis of the problem, was its call on the Church itself to play its part, through the establishment of the Church Urban Fund.[2] It happened that at the same time in 1988 I was trying, on behalf of the 'One Nation' segment of the Conservative Party, to breathe life into the concept of the active citizen. I was helped in this by being asked to preach in St Martin-in-the-Fields in London and around the same time to speak (uniquely for a Cabinet Minister) to a fringe meeting of the General Synod of the Church of England. Robert Runcie made this meeting possible, and I was deeply grateful to him for that. It seemed to me important that someone on the Government side should make it clear that the Church was entitled to express a view on matters of public policy – although when this intervention takes the form of criticism, bishops and others must expect to receive rebuttals and criticism in return, that being the nature of democratic debate.

The Church of England can claim to be the most effective collection of active citizens at work in our society. In many areas its strength is less than it was, but *Faith in the City* showed a determination and set an example which should be remembered and can be followed today.

Inevitably the Church conducts a continuous, though low-key debate within itself as to whether establishment helps or hinders its modern role; there is no measurable pressure for disestablishment from outside. Experience during the archiepiscopates of Robert Runcie and his successor show that the advantages continue to outweigh the occasional irksomeness of the link. For example, on the Wakeham Commission on the future composition of the House of Lords we examined carefully the role of bishops in the House of Lords. We thought that our Second

Chamber should go through substantial change, and I guess that this will happen in a future Parliament roughly on the lines which we proposed. But we were clear that the case for Church representation was so strong that it should survive, albeit with Anglican members reduced to allow for the representation of other churches and faiths. To take another issue, related to establishment, the Archbishop of Canterbury in his present role is needed to advise and sustain the monarchy during a period of difficult change.

The Church of England remains central to the life not of our whole country, but of hundreds of villages, towns and cathedral cities. It might be argued that this centrality is the result of architecture and history rather than of establishment and that it would continue, as it does in parts of Wales, even though the Church of England were disestablished. But establishment represents a fact in our present as well as our past, with which it would be rash to tamper. Perhaps more powerful still is the need for a voice to give an authoritative moral or spiritual view on the many difficult choices churned out by the processes of modern science and intellectual fashion. Of course this is largely a matter of personality. By force of personality rather than office Cardinal Hume became such an authoritative voice alongside, but not in place of, the Archbishop of Canterbury. But the See of Canterbury and its occupant retain an authority to pro-nounce, not just on behalf of Anglicans but on behalf of the nation as a whole. In this form establishment is not a relic of the past, but a response to a modern need. If there were no Archbishop of Canterbury leading an established church, the media might well be pressing for us to create one – or more probably they would select their own without any particular regard to legitimacy or the Church of England. As Robert Runcie found, this role of pastor and prophet to the nation is an extra-ordinary burden – but it is also an amazing opportunity.

During Robert Runcie's time the international side of the Archbishop's work grew formidably. He himself was particu-larly interested in the revival of Christianity throughout the former Soviet Union as Communism collapsed. Under his inspir-ation the St Andrew's Trust, operating out of Lambeth, raised money to bring likely priests and pastors to train in our universities. Robert himself spent many hours in establishing, re-establishing and making effective the contact that is once again now possible, particularly with the Russian Orthodox Church. At the same time he had to cope with the steadily increasing work of the Anglican Communion. This increase has continued under Archbishop Carey, and is the main factor for his decision to ask a group of outsiders to review, mainly for the benefit of his successor, the priorities of an Archbishop of Canterbury's workload. In gathering views and evidence for that review we have found notable ignorance in England, including in the Church of England, about the curious, indeed unique form of leadership which the Archbishop of Canterbury is expected to provide for 70 million Anglicans organized in 38 provinces. It can take the form of tumultuous, even chaotic, visits which attract huge crowds and enthusiasm, although barely reported here. It can require intervention in delicate disputes, though only by invitation, for no one is going to give the Archbishop of Canterbury any form of papal power over these autonomous Anglican provinces. But when there is a difficulty, for example, when the bishops left Rwanda at the time of the genocide, then the Archbishop is invited to provide a remedy. The organization and the finances of the Anglican Communion, and indeed of Lambeth, are not sufficient at present to sustain this role, a mismatch which is increasingly burdensome for the Archbishop himself. In return for this part of his work, however, the Archbishop of Canterbury acquires a degree of international knowledge and influence which again is hardly understood here. Every now and then, for example in the dramatic career of Terry Waite operating out of Lambeth on behalf of the Archbishop, we get a glimpse of what is involved. From time to time there are situations, even outside Church affairs, where the intervention of the Archbishop of Canterbury will be more effective even than that of the British Prime Minister or Foreign Secretary. The release of hostages is an obvious example.

Recently, with my colleagues on the Canterbury Review Group, we were invited to a meeting of Anglican Primates held in the United States. As the archbishops, in particular from the provinces of Africa, brought us up to date with the problems they were facing, we understood more clearly the worldwide importance of Canterbury. In the quiet hills of North Carolina we heard some dramatic examples. The Archbishop of Kenya had invoked the help of Canterbury in preventing government police from pursuing political dissidents into his cathedral. The Archbishop of Nigeria was delighted that on his recent visit George Carey had spoken out on the imposition of Sharia Law in the north of the country. From the account of the Archbishop of Sudan it seemed clear that if you wanted information and the possibility of influence over the course of the 18-year-old civil war in the south of that country, you might be advised to go to Lambeth before the Foreign Office. This role of leadership by invitation imposes a substantial and growing burden, and not just of money and staff. It requires difficult exercises of judgement, for example if the analysis of the Archbishop begins to diverge from that of the British Government.

In all these relationships Robert Runcie was keen on the concept of 'critical solidarity', a phrase originally coined by the late Giles Ecclestone, Secretary of the Church of England's Board for Social Responsibility. The Archbishop of Canterbury when he wishes can get close to the thoughts of those who make policy decisions in this country. No Sovereign, no Prime Minister, no Foreign or Home Secretary, no Vice Chancellor of a University or Chairman of a big charity is going to deny him access to their thoughts if he shows interest in a matter they are handling. But he can insert himself into their process without compromising his integrity and retaining the right to disagree. History, from Becket via Cranmer to Temple and Runcie, underscores this independence. There will always be room for argument as to whether the archbishop of an established church should be more critical or more solid in his comments on the public policies of the day. During his years as Archbishop of Canterbury, Robert Runcie showed that he understood the depth and intricacy of both parts of this concept. I believe that the balance which he struck between them was shrewd and principled.

2. Nudging the Government: Runcie and Public Affairs

DAVID SAY

> I long to be able to speak, while Archbishop, with men and women who stand outside the Christian Church. But I must stand also not at the edge but at the very centre of the Christian company as supporter and encourager.

This was how Robert Runcie saw his new role when he spoke at his enthronement in Canterbury Cathedral in 1980. He was about to take on what has been described as 'more than one man's job but which only one man can do'. He knew that in addition to being the diocesan bishop of Canterbury, Metropolitan for the Southern Province of the Church of England, Primate of All England, the acknowledged leader of the worldwide Anglican Communion, as well as an active participator in the ecumenical and inter-faith movements, he would be called upon to play a part in public affairs and in the political life of the nation.

Traditionally, archbishops had done this as both members of the House of Lords and through their confidential relations with members of the Government but, as Professor Adrian Hastings[1] has pointed out, it was William Temple, with his enormous concern for secular issues of all sorts, who began a shift in the life of the Church. He was, however, not a House of Lords man like Randall Davidson or Cosmo Gordon Lang. Instead, he preferred to act far more through public meetings, the chairing of conferences and the commissioning of reports. His successor, Geoffrey Fisher, whose interest in social issues was more limited, only partly followed the Temple lead, whereas Michael Ramsey, the heir to Temple in so many ways, took a remarkable lead in public affairs, not least in race relations. Harold Wilson, Prime Minister during part of his archiepiscopate, appointed him Chairman of the National Committee for Commonwealth

Immigrants, a very unusual appointment for an archbishop in modern times.

Runcie, on arrival at Lambeth, followed in the footsteps of Temple and Ramsey but he quickly realized the truth of Temple's own words that 'the Archbishop of Canterbury faced the responsibilities of a Cabinet Minister with the resources of a Headmaster'. So he quickly set about enlarging his staff and delegating responsibilities more than any of his predecessors had done. He appointed an experienced and trusted diocesan bishop to be his Chief of Staff and he encouraged his lay Secretary for Public Affairs to be as concerned with Government departments in Whitehall as with both Houses of Parliament. He was greatly assisted in this role for a number of years by John Lyttle, who had been chief officer of the Race Relations Board and later a member of the Police Complaints Authority, as well as a special advisor to Shirley Williams when she was a Cabinet Minister.

The House of Lords

Runcie soon made himself at home in the House of Lords where he found several peers with whom he had served in the Scots Guards during the Second World War, as well as other friends from the academic world and from the shires. He was very keen that the bishops as the Lords Spiritual should take as full a part in the work of the House as their diaries allowed. As the global dimension of his own work developed he himself found it more difficult to make time for Parliament. Nonetheless he made major speeches on the British Nationality Bill, on the Falkland Islands, on the fortieth anniversary of the United Nations and on the problems of the inner city, as well as a number on foreign policy issues.

He was jealous to preserve the role of the bishops as Cross-Benchers; they do not give (and are not expected to give) unswerving loyalty to any one of the main political parties. His attitude to the role of the bishops was that of 'critical solidarity'. This he believed should be the attitude of the Church to political authority more generally, because the Church's task is more than that of providing a sacred canopy overarching the social order.

In a speech on Church and State to the Coningsby Club in London in 1984 he set forth the principles which governed his intervention in political matters. First, there was the need to unpack the moral principles relating to any issue. Secondly, Christians must speak up for the poor and the powerless, both in body and spirit. His third principle was designed to be a reminder that no country is an island in more than the strictly geographical sense: that 'belonging' these days has an inescapable global perspective. The fourth principle he described as particularly Anglican. It was the responsibility to resist the mindless cults of unreason, both in religion and political life, and to strive for loyalty to truth.

He concluded this speech with a strong, positive affirmation:

I think the weaknesses of the Church can be exaggerated by those with a romantic view of its past, or ignorance of its present life. Diminished in numbers and distanced from Westminster, it is still the largest network of voluntary associations for social well-being in this country. Time and again it is this network, mostly staffed by the laity, that nudges the government. Above all, the Church still provides a nationwide meeting place for people of otherwise differing opinions to seek and find divine inspiration.[2]

The Falklands War

The two events which precipitated most sustained public controversy for the Archbishop were the Thanksgiving Service at St Paul's Cathedral after the conclusion of the Falklands War and the publication of the report of his Commission on the problems and need of the Church in Urban Priority Areas entitled *Faith in the City*.

When Parliament was recalled three days after Easter in 1982 to review the grave situation in the Falkland Islands following the invasion by Argentinian forces, the Archbishop spoke in the debate in the House of Lords. He said that he did so because he had the direct responsibility for the appointment and support of the Chaplain to the islanders, two-thirds of whom were Anglicans. He told the peers that he had the day before received a message from the Easter congregation in the little cathedral church, named after Canterbury Cathedral, assuring him that they were in good heart, steadfast and eager to maintain their link with him. In his speech he went on to emphasize the important principles which he believed to be at stake, namely, the overwhelming importance of international law and the right to self-determination of peoples, whether they be large or small in number.

In the following week Cardinal Hume issued a statement on behalf of the Roman Catholic Church urging the Government to take positive steps to bring about peace, while the British Council of Churches called urgently for a diplomatic solution to the dispute. When the time came for a national Falkland Islands Service at St Paul's Cathedral, at which the Archbishop preached, it was, like all such national services in recent years, an ecumenical occasion. Writing in *The Times* 12 years later, Alan Webster, the former Dean of St Paul's, emphasized the attitude of the other churches in the United Kingdom in consultation with whom he had planned the service.

> Their leaders [he wrote], Dr John McIntyre, Dr Kenneth Greet and Cardinal Basil Hume, were rock-like in their determination to avoid triumphalism and to pray for all those who had lost loved ones, whether they were British or Argentinian. Mourners comprised the majority of the congregation and one had only to meet the families in the Cathedral or to see their letters afterwards to feel that the tone of the service – thanksgiving, remembrance and reconciliation – was true to the Gospel.[3]

Runcie's sermon was not a 'victory sermon' but emphasized thanksgiving, prayer for all who had been bereaved and an aspiration for a better ordering of the world.

The Gulf War

Nine years later, after the invasion of Kuwait and when the threat of the Gulf War was imminent, the Prime Minister, John Major, invited both the Archbishop and Cardinal Hume to

Downing Street to tell them that diplomacy had failed and that there was no choice left but force. In his autobiography Mr Major records:

> Both churchmen recognised that a military strike was becoming inevitable but they were fearful of escalation and a loss of life . . . They gave me their public and private support and, in so doing, their reassurance that this would be a just war. Although I have never paraded my religion, their backing was important to me. I would have been uneasy without it.[4]

A few hours after the United Nations Deadline had expired Runcie broadcast the *Thought for the Day* on BBC Radio 4's *Today* programme. He quoted the martyr Dietrich Bonhoeffer. 'Bonhoeffer once declared that God is among us in our lives but not on any side'. 'And that', the Archbishop said, 'is an instructive Christian insight which helps to maintain our resources of compassion and mercy as we seek to do justice'.

A most significant report

Faith in the City is likely to stand as the greatest single achievement of Robert Runcie's primacy. 'It was a very characteristic achievement, for which he was both most responsible and least – in regard to details – clearly involved', wrote Professor Adrian Hastings in his biography of Runcie.[5] The report was the work of an Archbishop's Commission but from the outset it was more than a domestic undertaking, for its terms of reference included not only 'to examine the strengths, insights, problems and needs of the Church's life and missions in Urban Priority Areas', but also 'to reflect on the challenge which God may be making to Church and Nation'.[6]

The report made 38 recommendations to the Church and 23 to the Nation. It was the work of a group that was predominantly lay and highly professional. It was rubbished even before it was published both by politicians and by the press but the reaction was counter-productive as the nationwide publicity greatly increased the number of copies sold as well as the intensity of the public discussion aroused. A year later in a debate in the House of Lords on inner-city problems, Lord Scarman, the author of the earlier report on the Brixton riots, said,

> *Faith in the City* is the finest face-to-face analysis and description of the problems of the inner city and of other urban priority areas. In the long run it will take its place, I believe, as a classic description of one of the most serious troubles in British society.[7]

Archbishop-in-Synod

Runcie was the first Archbishop of Canterbury to come to office with experience, as a diocesan, of being a 'bishop-in-synod'. He had accepted government by Synod from the start and welcomed a development that allowed the clergy and laity to co-operate in church government in the way that the Hodson report *Government by Synod* proclaimed that 'theology justified and history demonstrated'.[8]

Under Runcie's leadership the House of Bishops began to have a more demanding agenda and to take a more prominent part in the General Synod. After one session at York, Clifford Longley commented in *The Times* that, 'what had emerged enhanced was the collective leadership and authority of the bishops'. As the Archbishop only has to chair the Synod on formal occasions he is able, if he wishes, to assume the role of 'Leader of the House' and this Runcie did by speaking fairly frequently and sometimes by undoubtedly influencing the voting in all three Houses. The members of the Synod, for the most part, paid attention to what he said because it was obvious that his speeches were well researched and carefully prepared. He evoked respect because he had the capacity to re-appraise his own position as, for instance, over the ordination of women, and also because on occasion he was ready to express a minority view, as he did in the memorable all-day debate broadcast by the BBC on the report of the Synod's working group on nuclear warfare – *The Church and the Bomb*. Runcie argued against the unilateral recommendations in the report because he believed that British unilateralism would not serve the cause of peace effectively.

The wealth ethic

Runcie was clearly sensitive to the rapidly changing scene in the world of communications and he went out of his way to make time for the press and the media. In 1989 he was interviewed by the Deputy Editor of *Director*, the magazine of the Institute of Directors, on the subject of wealth creation when he said that there was no automatic connection between wealth creation and a happy society. 'I resist the idea', he declared, 'that the only driving dynamic of society is self-interest'. He went on to say that the then government supported a view of society in which an individual's rights and duties were enhanced but, while he argued that this was part of the Christian ethic, the Church always balanced this with its understanding of Christians belonging to one another and making up the Body of Christ.

> That gives us a corporate dimension to our faith and ethics which is bound sometimes to be at variance with a highly individualistic approach. The Church puts as much of its energies and resources into building community life. It does so in its life of worship but also in its service, social and practical, to parishes, institutions and organisations throughout the country.

He said that one of the challenges sometimes presented to the churches – and particularly to the Church of England – came from that section of our political and commercial leadership which said, 'We have made the people wealthy; it's the Church's job to make them good'. That was not the Church's view of its task. Instead he roundly affirmed, 'It wants to make people godly. Godliness and goodness are not the same thing'. He made it clear that he was concerned that tomorrow's business leadership might feel less committed to community help and that he felt that the ties that existed between an older generation of achievers and the Church had been weakened. He sensed the danger of Pharisaic attitudes towards the unsuccessful.

It was sad that this long and thoughtful interview, reported at length in the *Director*, a magazine stated to be for 'decision-makers in business', was summarized in a press release under the heading 'Thatcher's Pharisee Society'. It was a particularly shameless example of media hyping to which, unfortunately, the Archbishop was all too accustomed.

The press and the Archbishop

Dr John Simpson, the former Dean of Canterbury, has written that Dr Runcie's archiepiscopate will in years to come 'be viewed as a time when the Church became central again in national consciousness'. Like many others he was grateful for 'the firm hand' of which the Archbishop had spoken in his Enthronement sermon in 1980 – 'a firm hand against rigid thinking, a grudging temper of mind and the disposition to over-simplify difficult and complex problems'.[9]

The fact that Robert Runcie took a prominent part in national affairs and, while supporting the government of the day in much that it did, never hesitated to oppose it strongly on issues like the Nationality Bill and the Immigration Bill, almost certainly led to him being attacked and belittled by journalists to an unprecedented degree. *The Tablet*, the international Roman Catholic weekly paper, in assessing Dr Runcie's achievements said with directness:

> The tabloid rottweilers have been hungry for his blood precisely because he will not endorse their own rotten values . . . this resistance to the humbug which masquerades as a lofty demand for clearer moral leadership is not the only reason why future historians will recognise Dr Runcie as one of the great Archbishops of Canterbury.

Criticism and denigration by the press was relentless and reached the point where former employees at Lambeth were being pursued in the search for evidence to fuel even more personal attacks on both Robert and Lindy Runcie, to cast doubts about their marriage and even to raise the possibility of their separation. In October 1986 the situation had deteriorated so seriously as to prompt several bishops into responding vigorously to the repeated attacks in the press. On the night before a meeting of the House of Bishops, the Archbishop dissuaded them from taking any action but the next morning, after a further attack, he agreed to the matter being raised when the bishops met. The House of Bishops passed a unanimous resolution which stated that it

> condemned the scurrilous and baseless attacks on the Archbishop of Canterbury and Mrs Runcie in the *Sun* and *Star* newspapers, entirely disassociating itself from the sentiments expressed in the offensive articles, reaffirming its confidence and thankfulness to God for the Archbishop's leadership and pledges its love and support to him and his wife in face of the personal distress these attacks must have caused them.[10]

Two years later 1988 the Lambeth Conference was anticipated by the British press with doom and gloom, to the bewilderment of bishops from across the world. But the Conference, which ended in a renewal of spiritual energy and fresh vision, was an undoubted triumph for both the Archbishop and his wife. Bishop John Krumm, a veteran American bishop, said,

> There is no question that Robert Runcie emerges from the Conference as a miracle worker. His sympathy and willingness to listen, his belief in the virtue of compassion and the importance of remaining in close communion with one another, has left his imprint upon this conference as perhaps no other Archbishop has ever done at a Lambeth Conference.[11]

Retirement years

Retirement gave Runcie greater opportunities for seeing his friends and for doing some of the things that he enjoyed most, but he was constantly in demand for public engagements and was tireless in speaking not only at memorial services but at anniversaries and celebrations of every kind. As a Life Peer he sat on the Cross-Benches in the House of Lords but his participation in debates was rare. He was a regular visitor to the United States and in his last years he undertook speaking engagements under the guidance of Dr John Harper, Chairman of the American Friends of Canterbury Cathedral, during which period he helped to raise two million dollars for the new Education Centre in the precincts of Canterbury Cathedral.

In 1991 he was nominated for the honorary post of High Steward of the University of Cambridge, an office which dates from 1418 and ranks second only to the office of Chancellor. He chaired the Faculty of Divinity Development Committee and helped in the fund-raising for a new building for the Faculty. In 1998 he cut the first turf and a year later laid the first brick, but sadly he died before the opening of the new building in West Road by the Queen in November 2000. On that occasion the large lecture theatre in the basement was inaugurated as the Runcie Room. Lady Runcie was present for the ceremony of dedication by the Bishop of Ely and for the hanging of a portrait of her husband in the room.

His style of leadership

Robert Runcie has sometimes been compared with Randall Davidson, Archbishop of Canterbury from 1903 to 1928. Canon Paul Welsby, author of *A History of the Church of England, 1945–1980*, has written that,

> this comparison holds insofar as, like Davidson, Runcie has been concerned to hold together the Church of England by weighing all points of view, refusing to capitulate to extremists and being shrewd enough to know when to speak and when not.[12]

Bishop George Bell, in his monumental life of Randall Davidson said that there are two kinds of leadership:

> There are those who are leaders of a cause on the success of which they stake everything they have; and all their efforts, all their acts are devoted to the achievement of their particular plan or their particular doctrine. Such leaders will drive forward as fast as they can and will cry aloud to their followers to make haste after them but there is another kind of leader who, having a charge entrusted to him and a body of people

at whose head he is placed, rather seeks to act as the interpreter of the best mind that is in them and to give it expression . . . Such a leader will guide and will show the way and he will teach and suggest but he will not be likely to lift his voice from the housetops and to cry aloud to the laggards to come on at full speed . . . He runs the risk of misrepresentation and is unlikely to win great popular applause but he is not on that account to be dismissed as an unsuitable kind of leader in dangerous and unsettled times.[13]

The leadership of the Church of England given by Robert Runcie, half a century after Randall Davidson, was never that of the leader of a cause. Rather he sought to bring out the best in those with whom he worked, to listen to what they had to say and to reach a consensus of opinion whenever possible. He was relaxed and cheerful in style and had the physical stamina to overcome all the incredible pressures of the local, national and international demands made upon him.

In an address to Members of Parliament at St Margaret's, Westminster, on the occasion of the Opening of Parliament in 1987, he spoke of the pressures in public life today:

I know myself something of these pressures – the pressure of living so much in the eye of the media that public image can become the puppet-master of private self; the pressure to give to public life more than can properly be spared by wife or husband or children and to make so many acquaintances that there is no space left for friends. The pressure of receiving so much criticism which is arbitrary or unjust means that one becomes impervious to or resentful of **all** criticism.[14]

John Habgood, who as Archbishop of York complemented Runcie's gifts so admirably, has emphasized Runcie's 'consciousness of history' and his 'love of style, especially in speaking'. He has said,

there was nobody better suited for the job available at the time and he had the stature for it. It was his bad luck that he had to do it during an exceptionally difficult period and that he was to some extent damaged by the vicious campaigns against him. As I saw him, he was a classic Anglican who managed to maintain his balance against all odds.[15]

At its meeting after the 1988 Lambeth Conference, the Anglican Consultative Council passed a resolution thanking Dr Runcie for his

patience, humour and fairness, for his pastoral care and for his personal spirituality. His quiet dignity without pomposity, his warm and gracious encouragement and his sensitive approach to fellow church leaders, have enriched the entire Anglican Communion and many others beyond its membership.

Robert Runcie was both a man of God and a man of the world. He had fought in battle and had been decorated for bravery and he had friends all round the world. This was borne out at the crowded Service of Thanksgiving in Westminster Abbey when the diversity of life represented in the congregation included some 60 peers, as well as 40 bishops, together with representatives of many sides of public life into which Runcie had entered with his inimitable enthusiasm and gifts of friendship. The great company of his friends united to thank God 'for his friendship, his love for family and friends and for the way he made each person feel special'. They also thanked God 'for his quiet prayerfulness, for his ability to laugh at himself and for his keen sense of the ridiculous'. Many of those present left Westminster that day also remembering his delightful smile and his loving embrace.

3. Facing Both Ways: Runcie's Social Vision

ERIC JAMES

When I first met Robert Runcie, in Cambridge in 1955, he had just been appointed Dean of Trinity Hall and the term – but not just the term – 'social responsibility' was far from him. It would, indeed, be another three years before the Church of England set up its Board for Social Responsibility; and – let's face it – Robert Runcie, both as Dean of Trinity Hall and as Principal of Cuddesdon, remained at some distance from the ecclesiastical bureaucracy of the Church of England. It was only when he became Bishop of St Albans in 1970 that he had to give his mind to social responsibility, as Church House, Westminster, conceived it. Then it became a major subject on which he had to exercise his episcope, his leadership as a bishop. However, before we wade into those deep waters, let us remind ourselves that Robert Runcie never was and never would be other than primarily a 'person person'. He would enjoy seeking out the right individual to be Social Responsibility Adviser for, say, the Diocese of St Albans and would never tire of giving his heart and mind and judgement to what that person had to advise. Yet there is more to be said than that about Robert Runcie and Social Responsibility prior to 1970 – much more.

You could not be brought up in Liverpool in the twenties and thirties with a Tate & Lyle engineer for your father and a Cunard hairdresser for your mother – with a father who would be totally blind by the time you were in your late teens – without, let us say, unformed ideas of social responsibility. Nor would such a school as the Merchant Taylors' Boys' School, Crosby, have its scholars ignorant of the social realities. Indeed, Robert remembered one of his Classics teachers at school – 'Joe' Parr as he was nicknamed: 'Joe' after Joe Stalin! – who had at least a temporary socialist influence on the young Runcie, so much

so that he would take home Left Book Club books. It was at
school one day that Robert said he thought about ordination
and pictured himself as a 'slum priest', after the example of
one of the local priests at St Faith's, Crosby, whom he rather
hero-worshipped.

Furthermore, I do not myself think that volunteering for the
Scots Guards in time of war – in time of a war that was under-
taken to defeat Naziism (and would involve Robert Runcie con-
fronting the realities of Belsen) – should be ignored nor, indeed,
be excluded from any consideration of Robert Runcie's 'social
responsibility'. Nevertheless, it would be fascinating to pursue
what particular aspect of social responsibility it was that caused
Robert 'to stay regularly' (I quote) at that time, at Rosa Lewis's
extraordinary Cavendish Hotel, Jermyn Street, W1! It was, of
course, this hotel which was the inspiration for the TV series
The Duchess of Duke Street and receives an oblique mention
in Evelyn Waugh's *Vile Bodies*.

When Robert returned to Brasenose College, Oxford, after
the war, we know that he took an interest in the Conservative
Party, of which he became College Secretary. We know too that
this brought him into contact with Margaret Roberts, better
known later as Margaret Thatcher. But he also joined the Social-
ists! The unkind would say that this is but the first example of
Robert Runcie's social irresponsibility: that his social responsibility would always have something of Mr Facing-Both-Ways
about it. I myself prefer to remember that when Christian Action
was founded in 1946 – the charity founded by Canon John
Collins, of which I was privileged to be Director for the last 17
of its 50 years – Robert Runcie chose to be at that foundation
meeting in Oxford Town Hall: on 5 December 1946. There
were 1600 in the Town Hall, about 800 in St Mary's Church
and another 600 outside. Bishop Bell of Chichester, Sir Richard
Acland, Barbara Ward and Victor Gollancz were the speakers
that night, alongside John Collins. There went out from that
meeting A Call to Christian Action in Public Affairs. Robert
Runcie supported Christian Action for all its 50 years. There
was no 'facing both ways' in that commitment of his. Indeed,
he encouraged me to be the Director of Christian Action while
I was still his Canon Missioner at St Albans. The first initiative

from Christian Action in 1946 concerned post-war reconcili-
ation with Germany. It meant a greatly increased response to
Oxford Famine Relief and to Save Europe Now. The Berlin
Philharmonic Orchestra was courageously invited to England.

In 1950 Robert Runcie was ordained to a curacy – All Saints,
Gosforth, Newcastle-upon-Tyne. No one who knew him personally could doubt the importance of his two years as curate of
All Saints, nor its relevance to social responsibility. He could,
of course, have done with being there longer but he learned a
great deal from the vicar, John Turnbull, and the people, from
the parish and the city. Dr Bill Pickering, in his *Social History
of the Diocese of Newcastle 1882–1982*, wrote:

> Turnbull was in the Noel Hudson mould, clear-minded, per-
> suasive, pastorally minded – of great courage. He inherited
> in 1947 a church where the paid choir delighted the congre-
> gation and the heart of the parish was the matins congre-
> gation, forty to sixty in number and largely comfortably off.
> Pew rents still survived. They would be ready to answer an
> occasional appeal for the funds of the Church Lads Brigade
> or Hospital Sunday, even readier for a choirboys' treat but
> the essential vision of the whole Church as the worshipping
> Body of Christ, bound together as one by a common faith
> and sacrament, was missing. As soon as he felt he knew his
> congregation through visiting, he called a Parish Meeting to
> which they came in good numbers and there, without delay,
> Turnbull put all his cards on the table. Much that he said
> was uncongenial at first to many of the people but he spoke
> clearly and with authority. Five more similar meetings were
> held, the promise was made that matins would not be discon-
> tinued without their consent, opposition was diminished and
> the Parish Communion was launched. At first the congre-
> gation stayed at sixty or seventy but this embraced most of
> the PCC and officials. It grew after each Confirmation until
> it settled at about 250–300 communicants – later it grew
> again.
>   Turnbull also implanted in All Saints the principles and
> practice of Christian stewardship, thoughtful planned sacri-
> ficial giving, in money and in time, which meant a vast amount

of organisation and visiting by both clergy and laity. This was reinforced by the setting up of some thirty house groups, each of ten or twelve people who thrashed things out together. All of this prepared the parish for the next big challenge – the building of proper churches at Kenton, Fawdon and Regent Farm – a formidable task made possible only by the co-operation of the whole congregation at All Saints. Not only were these churches to serve adequately the needs of an ever growing parish but the effort deepened the commitment of the All Saints' people, it made them outward-looking and preserved them from the danger of complacency. As each church was built the next testing step was taken; Turnbull encouraged the people in that area to transfer their allegiance to the new church. Many would not wish to do this for natural reasons but when John Turnbull encouraged you to do some-thing you usually ended by doing it. Only thus could the church grow. Perhaps one more thing should be said to clarify the picture. One was tempted to write off All Saints as a congregation of well-off people for whom life was easy but, in fact, by the time that Turnbull had been there for some time, the congregation was far more varied than that. A con-siderable proportion, it is true, of the professional and execu-tive classes, unknown in some parishes but also a fair proportion of people in more modest circumstances, to use a worldly phrase – clerks, artisans, poor people – all welded into the family and treated with equal honour. If the financial resources were still well above the average, so were the chal-lenges they accepted and successfully accomplished. Much similar work was being done elsewhere to which one would eagerly pay tribute if space were adequate but nowhere was so large an area covered in so deeprooted a manner – it was a golden chapter in parochial history.[1]

Westcott House liked to send its young men to the industrial north-east to serve their curacies. Robert Runcie knew he could never have gone to a better place. He revered its vicar for the rest of his life.

Few people would expect Robert's next phase – as Vice-Principal of Westcott House from 1953 to 1956 – to have much to contribute on the subject of social responsibility; but I have reason to think otherwise. I have already said that I first met Robert Runcie when he had just been appointed Dean of Trinity Hall and was about to leave Westcott House; but what he immediately asked me to do was significant. He asked me whether I would take on a group of students, whom he had been preparing for a visit which he was intending to lead in the vacation, to the parish of St Wilfred's, Halton, Leeds, where Ernie Southcott was then the colourful and energetic vicar.

Southcott based his ministry primarily on house churches, on a weekly parish meeting, and on the weekly Parish Communion – a colourful celebratory event with much lay participation. 'Let the Liturgy be splendid!' was one of Southcott's watchwords. In 1956 he published a book which would be widely read: *The Parish Comes Alive*. Denis (now Lord) Healey was then MP for South Leeds – thus Halton was within his constituency. He said: 'Ernie's Christianity was numinous and he impressed me more than any priest I have ever met'.[2] John Robinson had written an important article on 'The House Church and the Parish Church' for *Theology*.[3] It was significant that it was to this particular parish that Robert had wanted to take a party of a couple of dozen Cambridge students. In part, no doubt, it was because he was still wistful for northern parochial life; but it was also because in Newcastle he had learned the potential of the parish. In the end, he knew that the crucible of social responsibility in the Church of England must be the parish, and Ernie Southcott, in his house meetings and parish meetings, was using the parish as that crucible – for local, national and international concerns to be confronted in the light of the gospel. 'If we are alive to our responsibility for the person next door', wrote Ernie Southcott in the last chapter of *The Parish Comes Alive*, 'then we are more likely to see that next door to the next-door-but-one can lead us out to our responsibilities in Kenya and Johannesburg and Cyprus'.[4]

It was significant that when, after four years at Trinity Hall, Robert became Principal of Cuddesdon, he insisted he should also be Vicar of Cuddesdon – albeit a parish of less than a thousand parishioners. He had learned from John Turnbull – and from his friend Bill Vanstone (who would be Vicar of

Kirkholt, the Manchester housing estate, for 21 years, from 1955 to 1976) – that, to use Patrick Cowley's phrase: 'The Parish is the Passion'. I think it is also important for us to note that in 1962 Robert Runcie delivered the Teape Lectures in Delhi. He kept the Cambridge Mission to Delhi close to his mind and heart and, should anyone want to know the meaning of social responsibility, they could not do better than spend some time with the Brotherhood of the Ascension, this Cambridge Mission to Delhi, as in 1962 Robert Runcie did.

We are now almost ready to begin to make some evaluation of the social responsibility of Robert Runcie, bishop and archbishop. But it is, I think, important that we should first consider some of the changes and developments in the post-war world – not least in its thought – which caused the Church of England to set up its Board for Social Responsibility in 1958 and helped to shape its first years; for these were likely to be influences on Robert Runcie in his years of ministry before he was consecrated bishop.

It is difficult now to appreciate just how powerful the Church of England was in pre-war society – indeed, until relatively recently; but the secular society has now undoubtedly arrived; and the exercise of social responsibility is in some ways an example of the Church's response to its new situation. Until the mid-fifties, much of what the Church felt it needed to do in society could be summed up as 'Moral Welfare' – primarily with illegitimate children and their mothers and with prostitutes. After the war, however, attitudes rapidly changed. Social work became secularized and professionalized. With the development of the probation service and children's departments, the Church's moral welfare became relatively 'small beer'. In 1958, the Board for Social Responsibility was set up to 'promote and co-ordinate the thought and action of the Church in matters affecting family, social and industrial life'. Moral welfare was a relatively small part of that brief.

There had, of course, been conferences before the war which foreshadowed social responsibility – notably COPEC (Conference on Politics, Economics and Citizenship) in 1924. There was also the Christendom Group, the brainchild of Maurice Reckitt. There were also, of course, major Christian charities with concern for particular aspects of life and society: children, young people, the elderly, housing, etc.; but secular provision became of overwhelming importance. Major publications in the 1960s made plain that a new world had arrived. These included books like Bryan Wilson, *Religion in Secular Society*, 1966; Alastair MacIntyre, *Secularisation & Moral Change*, 1967; and David Martin, *Religion and the Secular*, 1969. It was within this secular, indeed increasingly secular, society that Robert Runcie was consecrated Bishop of St Albans on 24 February 1970.

Were it possible, I should like now to summon Canon Mike West, Industrial Chaplain in St Albans Diocese from 1969 to 1981, to be my first witness to the social responsibility of Bishop Runcie. Robert placed great confidence in Mike, and the Industrial Mission in St Albans was aware of and grateful for the Bishop's support. Sometimes he would meet with senior management in the diocese; sometimes, with trades union officials; sometimes there were, of course, problem situations which needed to be addressed directly.

Kodak at Hemel Hempstead, for instance, in 1970, was a non-union company, dealing only with its in-house Workers' Representative Committee. The Conservative Government's Industrial Relations Act 1971 gave all workers the right to be represented by a trade union. Kodak transformed the Workers' Representative Committee into the Union of Kodak Workers – unconnected with other trade unions. There was a small number of employees who had retained their membership of TUC unions while working for Kodak – particularly those in the printing section. In May 1973 this group was in dispute with the company about rates of pay for operating new equipment. They demanded that their union – the Association of Cinematograph Television & Allied Technicians (ACTT) should be recognized to handle this dispute. Kodak refused and a strike was the result. The Industrial Chaplain to Kodak got involved and began to develop the view that, if the workers had the right to be represented by a trade union, they had the right to choose which union. The Industrial Mission issued a statement to this effect. Kodak complained. To whom? To the new Bishop – who was embarrassed and, indeed, cross that he had not been consulted or kept informed about the public statement. Nor was

he wholly persuaded by the Industrial Chaplain's argument. In
public, however, the Bishop affirmed the Chaplain's right to
have an opinion on the matter, since both people's rights and
duties and their responsibility to express their views in public
were involved. There was, for a time, a real danger that Kodak
would suspend the Chaplaincy. This all happened just as I
arrived in St Albans Diocese as Canon Missioner. One of my
first assignments, much to my surprise, was to go to Kodak as
what the Bishop called his 'trouble-shooter'! It was he who sent
me. I am certainly not aware I did anything except to go and
listen to Kodak's management, to the Union representatives and
to the Industrial Chaplain. It was clear that the management at
Kodak were impressed with the fact that the Bishop had taken
them seriously and there was soon a settlement of the dispute
satisfactory to all sides.

Another rather different crisis situation reached the Bishop
via the Industrial Mission. It occurred in relation to the Hawker
Siddeley Aviation factory at Hatfield, where Mike West was
himself Chaplain. In October 1974 the company announced the
cancellation of its plans to design and build a new small airliner,
the HS146. This, of course, created a threat to employment on
the site, as this was the only new civil airline project then being
designed in Britain. The workers at Hatfield, organized through
their trade unions, began a huge campaign, both locally and
nationally, to persuade the company and the Government to
continue work on the aircraft. They lobbied Parliament, assisted
by the MP for Welwyn-Hatfield, Helene (now Baroness) Hay-
man. The Bishop wrote, via his Industrial Chaplain, to offer to
arrange a meeting between the unions and the members in the
House of Lords. This took place in a Committee Room in the
House on 21 November 1974. About 10 members of the House
of Lords, with aircraft interests, took part – including those with
pilot's licences, those with interests in airline companies and,
more generally, in the engineering industry as a supplier of parts
and components. Robert encouraged the shop stewards to present to the meeting both the potential of the new airliner and
the threat to employment in Hertfordshire if the programme
were to be cancelled. The meeting was enlivened when, after 40
minutes, the Bishop of Leicester, the then chairman of the Board

for Social Responsibility, who had been conducting prayers in the House of Lords, came into the meeting in full episcopal robes. 'Who is the man in fancy dress?' asked one of the stewards in a loud whisper. He had clearly not thought of Robert as being that sort of bishop! The campaign was a success. The Government provided a small amount of funding for design work to continue and, when the industry was nationalized in April 1977, the aircraft was re-launched as the BAe146 – the most successful airliner ever produced by the British aircraft industry.

I cite these two very different examples of social responsibility, both of which arose from industrial chaplaincy, not least because they so clearly contrast with the days of social responsibility limited primarily to moral welfare. In 1976 Robert Runcie appointed John Austin as the first Social Responsibility Adviser for the Diocese of St Albans. He had served in inner South London for over a decade and had been trained in Chicago in community development work. He would go on to be Director of the Board for Social Responsibility of the Diocese of London and, in 1992, would be consecrated Bishop of Aston, Birmingham. John Austin's appointment was a good example of Robert Runcie, the 'person person', making imaginative choices, not least in the field of social responsibility.

Robert, as a historian, enjoyed being Bishop of St Albans, not least because at its centre was a glorious Norman Abbey with 900 years of history, with a saint and martyr at the centre of that history whose legend goes back to the third century. Nevertheless, when he asked me to become his Canon Missioner in 1973, he said he was well aware that St Albans itself had a population of only 50,000 – albeit growing – whereas the largest town in the Diocese was Luton, with a population of 160,000 and with complex industrial problems. Next came Watford, with 80,000 people. Then there were the new towns, like Stevenage and Welwyn Garden City, with their particular problems. In the north of the diocese was the sizeable town of Bedford (74,000 people) which people were apt to describe simply as a 'market town'; in contrast to this, John Brown, a professor from Cranfield College of Technology, as it then was, had recently written a book calling Bedford 'The Unmelting

Pot'. He chose this title since the various races that had come to live there, who would often be working in the surrounding brickfields – Italians, Poles and, increasingly, people from the Caribbean – did not 'melt' together, either with each other or with the 'natives' of Bedfordshire, and vice versa. Robert wanted his new Canon Missioner to try to help the people of St Albans' Diocese to have a more realistic understanding of the Church's 'mission' in the last part of the twentieth century; his appointment of John Austin as Social Responsibility Adviser was another appointment to that end.

Both of us recall two particular issues relating to social responsibility which Robert Runcie was keen to set before the Diocese of St Albans – and not only the Diocese. The first was CRAC, the Central Religious Advisory Committee, which served both the BBC and the Independent Broadcasting Authority. When Ian Ramsey, Bishop of Durham, the chairman of CRAC, suddenly died in 1972 after chairing one of its meetings, the members – bishops, theologians, academics and people experienced in the world of the media – had to elect his successor. After consulting the Archbishop, Michael Ramsey, they elected Robert Runcie. He took over CRAC at a demanding time. The committee had been grappling with two major issues. The first was what was called 'the closed period' – an inheritance from the earliest days of broadcasting when no programmes at all were allowed on the air when people – according to Lord Reith – ought to be in church! Gradually the period had been abbreviated but many of the broadcasting staff believed that a breakout from the closed period was the only healthy way to better and more effective religious programmes. Not all the members of CRAC agreed.

The second major issue before CRAC at that time could be put in the form of a question: were the Christians who were responsible for religious broadcasting being either fair or charitable to Jews, Muslims, Sikhs, Hindus, Buddhists – people of other faiths – who were increasingly becoming citizens of this country? Robert was always particularly good at situations which required both compromise and respecting the conscience of the different and differing members of a body. He served for six years as chairman of CRAC, winning the respect of the broadcasting authorities and gaining a valuable knowledge of how the media professionals worked. He sought to share this knowledge and experience with the diocesan synod at St Albans and, indeed, with the Diocese as a whole.

Social responsibility, because so often it involves adopting – inescapably – a particular political stance, is also often identified with dramatic political speeches. Although Robert Runcie was undeniably a superb public speaker, he seldom made speeches on subjects of social responsibility which made the blood course in the veins! He was certainly no rhetorician where social responsibility was concerned. His speech as Bishop of St Albans in the General Synod on 4 February 1974 is a good example both of the manner of his speaking and of another important aspect of social responsibility which was his concern. It would be easy not to take very seriously a General Synod debate and, indeed, to ignore such a debate when the motion was

> to urge Her Majesty's Government to take steps to increase the amount of United Kingdom official development assistance to 1 per cent of GNP and to work for fairer terms of trade for the raw materials and processed products of developing countries and requests the Central Board of Finance to include in its future annual estimates a motion to contribute 1 per cent of its budget to overseas aid.

You can almost see the members of the General Synod escaping to the tea room or, if remaining, stifling their yawns!

Robert Runcie's speech that day is worth noting, not least because it is so characteristic of his approach – not only on social responsibility. He clearly was convinced the subject of the debate was important. Indeed, he had taken the trouble to put down an amendment to the motion before the Synod. He began with two quotations:

1. Dr Henry Kissinger: 'We have the ability to solve the problems of starvation in our day but we lack the will'.
2. The President of the United States, Richard Nixon, who told Church leaders: 'Help me to create an atmosphere in which more humane policies become possible!'

Robert then went on to say:

> I am concerned, particularly in that part of my amendment
> which refers to the World Development Movement, to balance
> our own support of development agencies with helping to
> create that sort of atmospheric pressure but, since I believe
> that clause (2) of the motion will meet with overwhelming
> objections, I am not happy about simply adding to the central
> board's budget and I am not happy about vague general
> encouragement. We need an appeal to the Church based on
> information and clear policy and in step with our fellow Chris-
> tians in the United Reformed Church and the Methodist
> Church, which are already acting coherently in this area along
> the lines of my suggestions . . .
>
> Our fellow Christians in the URC and Methodist Church
> have already been organising the type of annual appeal which
> is advocated by my amendment, linked to a particular day,
> such as harvest. The bulk of the proceeds from such an appeal
> have gone to Christian Aid and other developmental agencies.
> In considering the details of any scheme our Board for Social
> Responsibility would also have to consider the missionary
> societies as an arm of the development agencies, such as our
> appeal would suggest. Whether or not they do so, I believe
> that, like the URC and the Methodists, we should devote a
> proportion of a 1 per cent appeal – and the URC has a 1
> per cent appeal – to the World Development Movement for
> educational and political action. The URC appeal provides
> for 10 per cent of the result to be given to the World Develop-
> ment Movement. That might seem a reasonable proportion.
> There are those who, in a recent conference of people from
> the under-developed countries recommended a 25 per cent
> proportion but I do not want us to concern ourselves with
> details. I am anxious about the principle. I know that the
> Board for Social Responsibility is prepared to undertake work
> for this. It will be happy to consult and work out the details
> and the sort of appeal, literature and methods of payment.

No one could say that such a speech would 'set the world on
fire'. Robert was doing some of the 'donkey work', the drudgery,

on world development. It is, of course, possible, even probable, that he had been asked to speak in the debate not least because he was fast becoming noted for his responsibility in general. He was a 'safe pair of hands' and noted for his wise and responsible judgement. Giles Ecclestone was the Secretary of the Board for Social Responsibility at that time and it is almost unthinkable that Giles and Robert did not 'put their heads together' – and to good effect. Robert's amendment was carried.

Robert was not speaking then only in the General Synod. In November 1973 he had been introduced to the House of Lords. He spoke there only when he felt he really had something to contribute. Such speeches often concerned aspects of social responsibility. He was good at citing in evidence not only his own experience but the experience of others he had encountered at first hand. In a speech on the International Year of Disabled People he spoke most movingly:

> The disabled are a special care of the churches, because Christians cannot regard them as on the edge of society, or as objects of pity but as those who are at the centre of the discovery of depth in trust, love and sharing. I know a block of rather soulless flats in which lives a crippled man who cannot move from his room. The door is always open and it is with the so-called handicapped person that the desperate and lonely housewives, or the unloved children, can find attention and unselfish interest. The care of the handicapped always draws unsuspected qualities from those engaged in it and when you minister to others, they minister to you.[5]

In that same year, 1981, Robert spoke on the British Nationality Bill – or, rather, he spoke for its amendment. He ended his speech:

> I began by asking for a hearing from Church opinion. I conclude by reminding your Lordships that one of my greatest predecessors as Archbishop of Canterbury was Theodore of Tarsus. He might have had some difficulty in establishing his citizenship under the present Bill! However, in the seventh century he unified the English church and it is no exaggeration

to say that Theodore gave shape not only to the Church but to the nation, over against its separate kingdoms of those days. It is because this Bill will give shape and character to our future society that it is of such importance for us all. Though a Bill is needed, it may even be queried whether this is the right moment to bring it in ... It is at least my hope that this House will take its opportunity as a revising Chamber to remove some of those aspects of the Bill which have caused the deep concern that I have tried to voice.[6]

It was, of course, important that the Archbishop should make a major speech in the Lords on the Scarman Report on the Brixton disorders – 10–12 April 1981 – which he did on 14 February 1982, warmly welcoming the Report. The Archbishop had gone with seven Brixton clergy to see the Home Secretary not long after the Brixton disorders and he continued to be exercised in his mind as to how best the Church of England might respond to the situation – which, clearly, did not relate only to Brixton. In May 1981, I received a postcard from him, from (somewhat surprisingly!) Santiago de Compostela in Spain, which said:

bought a *Times* today and saw Clifford Longley on Inner Cities. It calls for a substantial letter from you. Nobody else knows so much about it. This is rather a fabulous place and I thought you would like a remembrance at the Shrine of St James!   Love: Robert

I did as my Archbishop commanded and the letter was published in *The Times* on 27 May 1981. In it I suggested that the Archbishop should appoint an Archbishop's Commission on the problems of Urban Priority Areas. I then wrote, as Director of Christian Action, to the Archbishop, asking that he should make a definite response to the suggestion. He replied, asking us to rough out some possible terms of reference for such a commission. The Scarman Report and the debates on it in the Commons and the Lords came early in 1982. Then, on 23 April 1982 the Bishop of Stepney – at the Archbishop's instigation – invited me to meet with the informal group of Church of

England Urban Bishops to get their response to my proposal. They agreed with it and by January 1983 the Archbishop had given it his approval. It took another six months to secure a suitable chairman for the Commission, Sir Richard O'Brien, to get a qualified secretary, John Pearson, seconded by the Government, and to secure appropriate ecumenical membership.

Perhaps the most valuable assessment of the Commission and its report *Faith in the City* is that of the Catholic theologian and historian Adrian Hastings, who said:

> Runcie's contribution to *Faith in the City* was, above all, a contribution to the calibre of its membership. If the job was to be done, it had to be done exceedingly well. All his sense of the necessity for perfectionism was here at work.[7]

In 2001, the Church Urban Fund, set up in 1987 as 1 of the 38 *Faith in the City* recommendations, still continues its work. The reverberations of the report are likely to continue for many years.

Some aspects of sexuality, such as the ordination of women, are treated more as matters of pure theology than of social responsibility – though sexual equality is, surely, a matter of social responsibility. The subject of homosexuality is less easily removed from social responsibility. Early in his archiepiscopate, Robert Runcie found himself having to declare unequivocally where he stood when the Gloucester Report on Homosexual Relationships was debated in the General Synod.[8] His speech on 27 February 1981 was one of his most important utterances. He congratulated the authors and hoped the report would promote more informed discussion. He said he believed those who were obsessive about so-called gay rights contributed to an unhealthy atmosphere and said:

> One of my rule-of-thumb tests for ordination would be that if a man was so obsessive a campaigner on the subject of homosexuality that it made his ministry unavailable to the majority of church people, then I would see no justification in ordaining him.

He sketched the main points of view within the Church:

1. Those who see homosexuality simply as a sin.
2. Those who see it as a sickness and feel it may be catching, yet have the obligation of exercising compassion.
3. Those who see it as a 'handicap' – a state with which people have to cope with limitations in which the fulfilment of heterosexual love and marriage are denied – though often through their handicap they can obtain a degree of self-giving and compassion which is denied to those not similarly affected.

Robert stated clearly: 'I do not believe that it is possible for anyone to be loyal to the Christian tradition and to see homosexual and heterosexual relations as having equal validity.' He did not say any more about the ordination of those who were homosexual. That was 1981. In the succeeding 20 years, society in general has undoubtedly come to regard homosexuals with much more warmth and understanding. Although there is still considerable 'homophobia', homosexuality is no longer the problem it was for most people of the younger generation. Homosexual actors and comics are now popular. The Church has moved but is still divided and maintains much prejudice within it under the guise of principle. Robert Runcie himself undoubtedly moved on the subject – but he saw his role when Archbishop as guiding the slowly moving Church and attending as much to its unity as to truth. One of the last telephone calls I had with Robert, in retirement, only a few weeks before his death, went like this:

> 'Eric. You're good at looking after gay priests. Will you look after one for me?'
> 'Yes, of course, Robert – but I've hardly ever heard you use the word "gay" before!'
> 'Well . . . we're all on the change now!'
> 'It's a bit late, Robert!'
> 'Yes', said Robert. 'It's a bit late.'

And, alas, it was.

As Archbishop, Robert Runcie was involved in social responsibility in a variety of ways. He addressed a great variety of bodies including Help the Aged, the National Association of Victim Support Schemes, the Abbeyfield Society, the Birmingham Community Relations Council, the Prison Reform Trust, the Thomas Coram Foundation, Oxfam. 'Today', he once reflected, 'I am at Oxfam. Tomorrow I shall be at the Bank of England!' The list of bodies concerned with social responsibility which he addressed over the years was vast. In his retirement and, as the end drew near, he had a particular concern for hospices.

There was, however, one charity which in his retirement came to have first claim on his energies. He was invited to be President of Emmaus UK. 'It seemed the right thing to support', he wrote. 'I have devoted much time to problems of the homeless in an increasingly prosperous society. Here was an opportunity to cease pronouncing and start being more practical.' 'Emmaus', he wrote on 8 December 1999, 'is one of the best things that ever happened to me in this decade . . .' At first glance it may seem an odd charity for Robert to have chosen. Intrinsically, there is little that is stylish in setting up self-supporting businesses for homeless people. Alternatively, it was straight down the middle of the Church Urban highway. It was also extremely practical, proven throughout the English-speaking world – a gospel-based secular charity founded by a tough and charismatic French priest and decorated Resistance hero whom Runcie much admired. It was also new to the UK, run by people in Cambridge he found amusing and enthusiastic, needing his networking skills. There was a curious appropriateness to the man who had been High Steward of the University of Cambridge since 1991 – since he had ceased to be Archbishop of Canterbury – becoming, as part of his stewardship, deeply involved in a Cambridge-based charity which could speak not only to town and gown in Cambridge but also to every level of society and every age group in the land.

At the end of the road for Robert Runcie – not least the road of social responsibility – was Emmaus.

4. Running the Gauntlet: Runcie and South Africa

DESMOND TUTU

In July 1988 the bishops of the worldwide Anglican Communion, with its 70 million members, came to Lambeth at the invitation of Robert Runcie, then Archbishop of Canterbury. This gathering was the latest in the series of Lambeth Conferences that normally meet at 10-year intervals. More accurately, we would be meeting not at Lambeth but in Canterbury at a residential gathering housed on the campus of the University of Kent. Many of us had misgivings about organizing such large jamborees; there were about 400 bishops, many with their spouses, consultants, observers and staff. We wondered whether all this money might not have been better spent in smaller regional meetings where even the most reticent would not be too intimidated and might get the opportunity to be heard. So there was then a healthy scepticism abroad about this massive get-together. We expected it to be dominated by a few articulate and even garrulous figures, present at an occasion when a significant number of bishops did not know English even as a second language. But, in all this, we were certainly not prepared for another extraordinary phenomenon, that was the almost vitriolic hostility of some of the British media in relation to Robert Runcie. These journalists predicted that the conference would be a dismal failure; they were proved wrong. The conference turned out to be a resounding success.

One could say at least two factors contributed to this happy result. The first was an innovation endorsed enthusiastically by the president of the conference, the Archbishop himself. This was the decision to divide the conference participants into small groups which met throughout the two-week duration of the conference for daily Bible study, prayer and discussion. In these groups everyone had a chance to speak because we had been asked to bring our dioceses, as it were, with us to the conference. So we each shared our experience, I believe at a profound level, as we told of our frustrations, challenges, joys and accomplishments while also providing a setting in which we could describe our particular countries, their histories and their peculiar situations. Our praying together for one another became increasingly more meaningful as we carried in our hearts the needs and joys of the churches and peoples of each member of our group. We came to know each other very well over that fortnight. I still carry in my intercessions package a picture of some members of our group, a picture that was taken in 1988. Two or three in that picture have gone ahead of us – Daniel Zindo of the Sudan, John Walker of Washington DC and Stanley Booth-Clibborn of Manchester have since died. I still try to intercede for my brothers as I look at the photograph; I know that many new friendships were made then.

Being divided into small groups meant that when we went to the larger sectional meetings and the plenary sessions small group members were now no longer strangers and aliens but in a real sense close members of an intimate household. Even when we held opposing views on controversial issues we tended to speak eirenically knowing that we were speaking to close members of the family rather than to hostile unknowns. Those small groups made that Lambeth – that was a universal verdict; even the sceptics were won over and supported enthusiastically the holding of another jamboree 10 years later. Since then, the small discussion/prayer group formula has come to be a regular feature of many diocesan and provincial meetings, certainly in the Church of the Province of Southern Africa and undoubtedly elsewhere too. Robert Runcie must be given the credit for an aspect of the life of the conference which made such a significant contribution to its success. Just as the captain of a winning side gets plaudits for the team's success, so at Lambeth 1988; it happened during his time as head of the Communion. The small groups were used to great effect in the succeeding 1998 Lambeth Conference.

The second factor that led to the success of the conference was Robert Runcie's presidency of the entire conference. He was friendly, warm and affirming of others and had the happy knack of making the apparently most insignificant and most unprepossessing of us feel important. He made us feel we really counted, and that whatever our views, for him they were important and were weighed very carefully. He was an excellent facilitator, both in the preparatory meetings leading up to the Lambeth Conference and in the daily meetings of the Steering Committee during the conference itself – these meetings assessed how things were going and suggested suitable adjustments to the programme. Robert had an amazing ability at achieving consensus; no one felt overridden nor would they go away with their nose out of joint. That was quite an achievement remembering the bewildering diversity represented among the conference participants, in terms of culture, language, race, theological viewpoint and church tradition. This is so typical of the Anglican ethos where divergent and other contradictory views exist cheek by jowl alongside each other. It was a mark of Robert's gifted and sensitive leadership that hardly anyone was left disgruntled, disillusioned or hurt.

Robert Runcie might have come across to some as indecisive; that is an unfortunate conclusion to draw. Robert was a thoughtful theologian who did not rush to cosy conclusions. He was very wary of facile dogmatisms that might offer simplistic answers to complex questions and which therefore tended to be exclusive of different points of view. He was very aware that the genius of Anglicanism has been precisely in the avoidance of too quick a determination that it is a matter of either this or that, instead of the more taxing approach which attempts to hold together both . . . and I recall when I first went to King's College, London, as a student in the 1960s being fascinated by the fact that most of my teachers seemed desperately keen to avoid providing us with the 'right answers'. Instead they were concerned to cultivate in us the habit of assessing the available evidence and opting for that conclusion which seemed to make the most sense of the evidence. I had just arrived from a South Africa where it appeared that the *raison d'être* of education was to teach students not so much how to think as what to think. There had been a clear belief in South Africa at that time that there were without doubt the right answers, which issued from the prevailing orthodoxy, and woe to those who might not want to toe the particular official line; we appeared to have confused disastrously the authoritative and the authoritarian. King's, London, was like a breath of fresh air after the claustrophobia of politically correct unquestioning, uncritical thinking. One of our Old Testament teachers, Professor Peter Ackroyd, summed up this British academics' allergy to dogmatism in a phrase he was wont to use after evaluating the pros and cons of this or that question: 'it is not unreasonable to suppose'. Robert Runcie was an embodiment of this principle. Far from being a failing, as those who pilloried him seemed to think, it was one of his most important qualities and one which qualified him so eminently to be the leader of a body I had characterized as being somewhat untidy (in its ways) but ever so loveable. He was able to hold together groups belonging to disparate cultures and viewpoints because he was so able to see the wood but not forget the trees.

This meant that a conference which had widely been predicted as being doomed to failure actually turned out to be a scintillating success, much to the chagrin of a somewhat bemused section of the British press. Someone they had regularly pilloried as gormless, with no backbone, too frequently sitting on the fence, was hailed by his peers. Quite unusually at the final plenary session of the conference the primates of the various provinces called the Archbishop of Canterbury to join them at the podium and standing around him read a resolution acclaiming his excellent leadership of the Communion in general and of that conference in particular. We pledged our support for him and our deep loyalty and affection for him too. At the end, the whole conference rose as one to give Robert Runcie a richly deserved standing ovation. We were letting the world out there know the esteem in which a revered and much-loved leader was held by those who looked up to him for support and leadership. The success of the conference proved to be a substantial 'one in the eye' for some acerbic and nitpicking individuals within the British media. Archbishop Robert was clearly deeply moved by all that took place.

I recall that when the name of his successor, George Carey, was announced, some papers gloated that mercifully there was now going to be a Christian in Lambeth Palace. How vicious can you get? Archbishop Carey's honeymoon period with a friendly media did not, unfortunately, last long. He and his family had to run the same gauntlet of vicious and hostile reporting that had been Robert Runcie's lot. This is a very odd phenomenon, this obsession of certain journalists in watching the reputations of prominent people biting the dust and being shown to have feet of clay.

In a way, this tribute is back to front. I have begun where I should really be ending. But I wanted to refer at the outset to the attributes of his leadership at their most public and most spectacular before I illustrated them in his dealings with our South African churches and with me personally. The next portion of this essay is then largely autobiographical. I hope it will reinforce the picture painted of Robert Runcie in the first part as the antithesis of the wishy-washy, namby-pamby, feckless parody that was constantly being vilified by part of the British press.

We in South Africa and I in particular experienced a side of that Archbishop's ministry little reported in the press. I was General Secretary of the South African Council of Churches from 1978 to 1984. During that period we were constantly under fire from the South African apartheid Government, being harassed throughout, while some of our staff would be detained without trial and kept in solitary confinement. We were targets for the Government-supporting electronic and print media – they were effectively propaganda instruments for a government that had identified the council as public enemy No. 1. Our council ran community development programmes in the rural areas, and provided scholarships enabling a number to gain tertiary education when they would otherwise have been roaming the streets. It was not these that riled the Government. What really got their goat were the projects which provided legal defence for trials of victims of the political process, whom the Government regarded as terrorists. Also unpopular was the support which the council gave to the dependents of political prisoners and detainees. Our programmes enabled family members to visit their relatives in maximum security prisons all over the country – the most notorious being Robben Island where people such as Nelson Mandela were incarcerated. We were accused of aiding and abetting enemies of the state and of being involved in subversive activities. The Government clandestinely set up 'front organizations' as rivals, and other 'patriotic councils' such as the Christian League. These spewed forth anti-SACC and anti-Tutu material, accusing the SACC of committing that most heinous of crimes, mixing religion with politics. The South African Government had managed to pull the wool over the eyes of most Western governments. It was involved in a massive campaign aimed at convincing the so-called free world that South Africa was the last bastion of Western civilization against the depredations of a rampant communism famously described as the 'evil empire' by US President Reagan. Sadly the West swallowed their propaganda hook, line and sinker.

Of course, the Government would have subverted their own position had they taken direct action against the SACC, a Christian organization; such action might have included banning the council. As it turned out, the apartheid regime did not balk at taking direct but covert action, as we found out later in the evidence that was brought before the Truth and Reconciliation Commission. An assassination attempt was made on Dr Frank Chikane, one of my successors as General Secretary of the SACC and now Director General in President Mbeki's office, by dousing his clothes with a poisonous substance. He fell desperately ill – luckily in the USA at a university where someone was doing research on precisely that substance, and that person was able to suggest effective countermeasures. Then there was the incident when a former apartheid Minister of Law and Order confessed that it was the police dirty tricks outfit that was responsible for the bombing of Khotso House, the headquarters of the SACC. When it happened, this man had had the gall to announce at a press conference that this outrage was undoubtedly the work of that terrorist organization, the ANC – Law and Order indeed!

The regime chose a clever ploy; they set up a judicial commission to investigate the SACC. This was the so-called Eloff Commission which the Government hoped would be able to rake up enough dirt about the council to persuade our friends overseas not to touch us with a barge pole and not to offer financial support. Since virtually all our budget was met by these overseas financial contributions, the SACC would have folded up without these. It was diabolically clever.

When the Truth and Reconciliation Commission began its public sittings, I telephoned some of our friends in the church organizations that had supported us in the UK, USA and Europe, to suggest that they might send delegations to come and testify before the commission. One of the allegations we had to answer was that we were really just puppets manipulated by these sinister overseas agents who supported 'that Marxist organization' the World Council of Churches. We were, it was claimed, a classic case of the one paying the piper calling the tune. We wanted our friends to come and refute this. They could do so by pointing out that we were controlled by the National Conference, whose members were appointed by the SACC member churches and organizations; this meant that we were answerable to that conference annually and to the executive committee elected by that conference. Between sessions of the conference we were completely autonomous. The reason that our partners supported us without determining our programmes was that we belonged to this remarkable thing, the Church of Jesus Christ, where if one member suffered the whole body suffered with that one member, and if one member prospered then all prospered.

It was quite exhilarating to belong to the Church, and our sisters and brothers in other parts of the world really brought ecclesiology alive for us. Perhaps it is ultimately only for those who are having a rough time, who are persecuted, and who are suffering that the Scriptures really do come alive. For at the heart of the gospel is the cross and we understood a little better than those who lived unmolested just how true it was that unless a grain of wheat falls to the ground and dies it remains alone, and indeed that if God is for us who can be against us?

In the book of the prophet Zechariah is a vision of a restored Jerusalem which will be so populous that it will not have conventional walls. Instead Yahweh promises that he will be as a wall of fire surrounding the Holy City. We had experienced being upheld, sustained and protected by a like wall of fire represented by the love, prayers and support of our sisters and brothers in other lands. Ultimately we were to score a spectacular victory over the awfulness of apartheid but this victory would have been impossible without that support and we are deeply thankful for it all. I recall once speaking to a nun in New York and asking her to describe her life as a solitary to me. She told me that she lived in the woods in California and her day began at two in the morning and that she regularly prayed for me. I mused to myself, 'Hey, here I am being prayed for by name in the woods in California at two in the morning – what chance does the apartheid Government stand?'

So we called on our friends and they really did us proud. They responded enthusiastically, sending delegations of top church officials from Norway, Denmark, Germany and the USA. Not to be outdone, Archbishop Runcie put together, at remarkable short notice, a high-profile delegation, including Terry Waite, to represent the Anglican Communion. The apartheid regime was hoisted on its own petard with a vengeance. Far from not wanting to touch us with the proverbial barge pole, all these top-notch leaders came to fraternize during one of the busiest weeks in the Christian calendar, Holy Week. They could not have been more enthusiastic in their support and the South African Government ended up with very considerable egg on its face. Archbishop Runcie announced that I was a Bishop in the Anglican Church and to touch me would be to touch the entire Anglican Communion. That was heart-warming stuff which did wonders for the morale of those who were frequently feeling they were reaching the end of their tether in the anti-apartheid struggle. The Archbishop was nailing his colours quite firmly to the mast and there was no wishy-washiness about it. In the end the Eloff Commission produced nothing but a damp squib.

On another occasion I was visiting France when the Pretoria Government made dire threats about what they would do to me on my return home. Archbishop Runcie arranged a media conference at Lambeth Palace where he made great play about having appointed me his personal emissary to His Holiness Pope John Paul II to carry to him a copy of the stamp commemorating their joint visit to Ghana in West Africa. He was signalling to the South African Government that I was no small fry and they should be very careful what they did to me. It was a high-profile assignment that sought to make me untouchable. On that

particular occasion, Robert Runcie had had a painful session
with the dentist but did not let that stop him carrying out this
appointment. He was still bleeding during the press conference,
such was the nature of his personal commitment to South Africa
and to freedom. Not long after that he provided me with a
venue in Lambeth Palace where I was able to meet with the
then President of the ANC-in-exile, Oliver Tambo. The South
African Government would be none too pleased, nor was such
action likely to have endeared the Archbishop to the British
Prime Minister, who supported President Reagan's disastrous
'constructive engagement' policy and who very firmly opposed
our calls for sanctions against Pretoria. The 'Iron Lady' showed
her colours in the struggle against apartheid by dismissing Nelson Mandela contemptuously as a terrorist. Robert Runcie was
thus certainly not currying favour with the powerful but aligning
himself with the divine bias in favour of the poor, the powerless
and the oppressed.

We met up with the Archbishop again in Vancouver in
Canada at the World Council of Churches' General Assembly,
held there in 1983. While strolling across the lawns of the local
university, he surprised me by suggesting that I had, as it were,
paid my ecumenical dues through my Secretaryship of the
SACC and that it was time I returned to being a diocesan
bishop. I have not shared this before publicly; he said he could
help by offering the then Bishop of Johannesburg, Timothy
Bavin, an English see. Bishop Bavin was much loved and a
courageous leader in South Africa and I learned a great deal
from him when I served as his dean. To cut a long story short,
he was offered and accepted the see of Portsmouth in England.
That created a vacancy in Johannesburg but it could not, of
course, guarantee my election. As it turned out the diocesan
Elective Assembly was deadlocked and the election was then
left to the Synod of Bishops. Before the Synod met I was awarded
the Nobel Peace Prize for 1984. The bishops elected me to
succeed Timothy Bavin. Leah and I were at General Theological
Seminary in New York when this happened. En route to Oslo
for the 10 December prize-giving ceremony we stopped over in
England. Robert invited us to stay in the Old Palace at Canterbury and arranged a wonderful service of thanksgiving and

celebration in a packed Canterbury Cathedral. Terry Waite represented His Grace in the ceremonies in Oslo.

Throughout all this time, the situation was getting grimmer in South Africa. We were becoming experts at conducting funerals as the security forces laid into defenceless protesters; they had virtual carte blanche in the use even of live ammunition. Almost always they would react violently to mourners at funerals. Thus we knew a funeral would be the cause of more deaths and so further funerals would lead to more deaths, rather as we have been seeing happen more recently in the Middle East. Increasingly we were being harassed and attacked by the Government. Robert Runcie again demonstrated both his solidarity with us, and that of the Anglican Communion, in our dire straits in an incarnational manner. He sent Keith Sutton and Terry Waite on at least two occasions to be his presence in our darkness and gloom. He cared not only by word but most eloquently by deed. This did not make him the blue-eyed boy of our Government nor did it serve to endear him to Mrs Thatcher.

My enthronement as Archbishop of Cape Town was regarded as an important moment both in the life of our church and for the Communion as a whole. All my predecessors had been whites and our country was in the throes of unprecedented harsh government under the apartheid regime's policy. There was a new spirit of resistance among the oppressed and their white allies. In 1986, the release of Nelson Mandela was still four years away and so, to mark the significance of the enthronement of a first black archbishop, the Archbishop of Canterbury himself, and several other Primates from all over the Communion attended. It was a wonderful celebration. Robert Runcie preached at an out-of-doors service after my cathedral enthronement and he did not mince his words.

He was there with us through thick and thin. He was a wonderful support with a huge sense of fun and apt to tell stories against himself. He endeared himself to many and so it was not at all surprising that two former archbishops from Africa attended his funeral in the Abbey at St Albans, which was full to overflowing. Many, many more were present at the Memorial Service in Westminster Abbey. Robert was a most courageous man, and only a week or so before his death presided at the funeral of Peter Moore, a former dean of St Albans and a good friend. In the early 1980s he was prepared to run the gauntlet of the national mood of patriotic fervour after the Falklands War. He reminded his congregation in St Paul's Cathedral that there were widows and orphans on the other side whom Christians did well to remember, thus ruffling many Establishment feathers. In due course, a conscientious biographer will give a fair and more accurate assessment of this exceptional man. We experienced him as a wonderful pastor and leader at a very difficult time in the history of South Africa and we are glad he was on our side. One day we shall all realize we had a great man in our midst.

PART TWO

An Archbishop's Loves

5. 'I'm Robert, what's your name?': Runcie and the Anglican Communion

MARY TANNER

There is a great deal of material available to document Robert Runcie's view of, and relationship with, the Anglican Communion during his time as Archbishop of Canterbury – sermons given on visits to various parts of the Communion, addresses to the General Synod of the Church of England, and presidential opening speeches to the meetings of the Anglican Consultative Council and the Primates' Meeting, as well as reminiscences of staff who worked closely with him in his relations with the Communion. But it is the opening address to the 1988 Lambeth Conference that provides the best clue to his understanding of the nature and purpose of the Anglican Communion.[1] His biographer, Adrian Hastings, recognizes this in the chapter he devotes to Runcie and the Anglican Communion.[2] In his opening address Runcie shows that his understanding of the Communion was inseparable from his understanding of the one, holy, catholic and apostolic Church, and from the call for the Church to be sign and sacrament of the unity of God's Kingdom in a broken and hurting world. He begins and ends with the vision of the new Jerusalem, the heavenly city, where the leaves of the trees are for the healing of the nations. In the light of that biblical vision he reflects on the threefold themes of Anglican unity, ecumenical unity and the unity of all creation, bringing out the inextricable relation between them. He was convinced that Anglicans should never make the Anglican Communion an end in itself. The churches of the Communion he reminded again and again have never claimed to be more than one part of the one, holy, catholic and apostolic Church. Anglicanism has, as he put it, 'a radically provisional character which we must never allow to be obscured', it should not be 'permanently canonised'. 'We are a provisional necessity because of the frailty of human nature'.[3] His understanding of Church history, his knowledge of the fathers, and his experience of dialogue with other churches, especially his chairmanship of the Anglican–Orthodox dialogue, provided the rationale for his understanding of the place of the Anglican Communion in the purposes of God. We might say that Runcie's priorities were God's kingdom, God's world, God's Church, and only then the Anglican Communion as a provisional embodiment of the Church. This was the understanding he set out at length towards the end of his archiepiscopate in 1988, but it was already hinted at in 1980 in his Enthronement Sermon.[4] There he acknowledged that one task which would exercise much of his time in the years ahead was to get to know the Anglican Communion. At the same time he was clear that this concern for the Anglican Communion and its unity could not be separated from a concern for the visible unity of the whole of God's Church, for Christians will not speak with the authority of Christ until they speak with one voice: effective witness to world peace and to social justice is hampered by divisions. Here in 1980, as in 1988, he showed that his concern for the Anglican Communion was bound up with his concern for the unity of all Christians, and was related to God's intention for the whole human race. It is not possible to do justice to Robert Runcie's understanding of the Anglican Communion without seeing it in this widest perspective: God's Kingdom, God's world, God's Church, his conviction that the Anglican Communion was a provisional embodiment of that Church, and his concern for the unity of all Christian people.

When Runcie became Archbishop of Canterbury rapid changes were already taking place in the Anglican Communion. The balance had shifted from North to South, with more of the 70 or so million Anglicans living in the South than in the North. English was the second or third language for the majority. There was a shift taking place also in the visibility and role of women in the life of the member churches, with the rise of the radical feminist movement in the United States whose influence was being more widely felt. As Runcie himself reflected, the Communion was no longer the church of the middle class allied to the prosperous Western world.

At his enthronement he spoke of his determination to get

to know the Communion at first hand. He knew the value of friendship and of identifying with the needs of others.

> When you are a friend to everyone, whether they belong to your group or not, when you have felt suffering, poverty and sickness, not necessarily in your own person, but by being a friend to those who suffer, then you are led into a depth of love which the hard-boiled never glimpse or attain.[5]

His travels were extensive. His first visit was to the enthronement in Bukavu of Archbishop Ndahura. Runcie was struck by the great difference between the simplicity of that enthronement, with no cathedral, no trumpet and without the encumbrances of the English tradition, which he seems to have wistfully envied. He saw his task as both to share from his English experience but, more importantly, to listen and learn what this new church had to tell about personal discipline and sacrifice and the fresh joy of being new followers of Jesus.[6] At the enthronement of the Archbishop of Uganda in 1984 he talked of the long line of martyrs from Thomas Becket to Janani Luwum saying, 'We cannot forget that to share in Christ's agony is to share the joy of his risen life.'[7] For him that was the key to the call to reconciliation and costly forgiveness of the horrors of that country's past. He encouraged Christians in Uganda to recognize the power of their witness in the rebuilding of the country. This was only one example of the many occasions where Runcie showed an ability to enter the local situation and relate it to the central message of the gospel. Wherever he went in Africa, Latin America, Australia, India, Japan, China, the Middle East, he took great trouble to understand the local scene and to build friendships.

Between 1980 and 1988 the number of provinces increased from 23 to 28 and the profile of the Anglican Communion as a worldwide Communion of churches was heightened. Partly as a result of his own determination to build friendships, the relation with the post-denominational church in China was developed and Bishop Ting was invited to the 1988 Lambeth Conference. The Archbishop also took a personal interest in the churches of the Indian Sub-Continent and was keen that the relationship which had been weakened when the Church of South India was formed in 1947 should be re-established. He visited South India in 1987 hoping to welcome the church back into 'communion', but an unfortunate debate in the General Synod of the Church of England on the eve of his departure counselled against such recognition because a few presbyters were still living who had not been episcopally ordained. It was a fine point which, in spite of his strong commitment to catholic order, disappointed and infuriated him with its apparent meanness of spirit. However, by the time of the 1988 Lambeth Conference the Archbishop was able to welcome bishops of these Indian Churches as full members of the Conference, in communion with the See of Canterbury. At the meeting of the ACC in 1990 he claimed that these churches 'enlarge the boundaries of our Communion . . . and are signals of our ecumenical vocation'.[8] It is hard to overestimate the importance of this event both for the Communion and for the ecumenical future. The Communion's ever greater inclusiveness and universal dimension was never for Runcie a matter of empire building but rather to be marvelled at as a window into that even greater diversity in unity that God intended for the catholic Church in this world. After eight years of travelling around the Communion he was filled with enthusiasm for what he had seen and heard, especially for the people he had met at the local level.

> I think of a hispanic 'street' celebration of the eucharist on the West Coast of the USA; of the consecration of four new churches on one boiling hot day in the outback of Australia; of the indomitable enthusiasm and valour of the Church of South Africa at Archbishop Desmond's enthronement; of the beauty and reverence of worship in Japan; and of the fresh idealism of young Anglicans at their meeting in Northern Ireland.

And jokingly he continued:

> So I have to say with some vigour to the British press, the Anglican Communion is not about to dissolve. And to the Church of England Synod that it is a little too early to be taking the covers off the lifeboats and abandoning ship.[9]

While addressing the bishops at Lambeth, much to the concern of his staff for the lateness of the hour, he departed from his prepared text to intersperse his theological discourse with some remembered person or circumstance from a visit to one or other province. He knew at firsthand the hardships experienced in many provinces, 'you come with wounds humanity cannot by itself heal – South Africa, Uganda, Sudan and Ethiopia, Korea and Sri Lanka, Nicaragua, Jerusalem and the Middle East, Ireland'. All of this confirmed the bishops present in their view of Runcie as having the care of the Communion of churches in his heart. This had much to do with the eventual outcome of the crisis over the ordination of women. Here was an archbishop who could enter into the experience and pain of the other and see things as others saw them. Here was an archbishop who didn't have all the answers but was prepared to wrestle with questions within the diversity of the Communion.

Of all his relations with the provinces it is perhaps that with South Africa which demanded most of him. Runcie was passionate in his concern for justice, 'justice tempered with mercy, and applied with humility'. From the beginning he looked to support the people of South Africa in their struggle against apartheid. He sent a small team to give evidence to the Eloff Commission who were enquiring into the activities of the then Bishop Desmond Tutu and the South African Council of Churches, a body that was in the forefront of the struggle against apartheid. In 1986 he attended the enthronement of Archbishop Desmond Tutu and preached at a concelebrated Eucharist in a stadium in Cape Town, aware that the whole world was watching. He acknowledged that those in the West who had done much to create the present tragic situation must be ready to repent and change and make sacrifices. 'I come', he said, 'to tell you in their name that we support you in your struggle to create a united South Africa out of the divisive forces that hold you in their grip.'[10] His hope was for a future for blacks and whites together. Using the words of Nelson Mandela he championed those who were against either white domination or black domination and who have cherished the ideal of a domestic and free society, a happy place for all peoples. To see Robert Runcie and Desmond Tutu together it was impossible not to be struck by the mutual admiration and deep affection they had for one another. In spite of his own illness Archbishop Desmond attended the funeral service of his archbishop in a wheelchair. There must have been times when Tutu longed for a bolder stand to be taken by the Archbishop of Canterbury against apartheid and a stronger support for the use of sanctions. With the Thatcher Government in power, however, and with the British press always eager to criticize, it was not easy for him to feel anything other than tension in the political arena. Nevertheless, under his leadership on the issue of South Africa, as on the plight of inner cities, the Church of England came to be recognized as the most effective critic of the Thatcher Government.

The other Communion matter that dominated the second half of his time at Canterbury was the fate of his Secretary for Anglican Affairs, Terry Waite. The tiny Iranian diocese found all its leadership, lay, clerical, both Iranian and expatriate in prison. The Primate of the Province in exile appealed to the Archbishop of Canterbury for help. Terry Waite had done much to draw attention to the plight of South Africa and Namibia, and requests for help from him were difficult to refuse. The original request came through the Episcopal Church of the USA to help the hostages in Lebanon. There is no doubt that the Archbishop was wanting to help nor was there any doubt that on the last visit he was less than happy for his Secretary for Anglican Affairs to leave. What happened is well known, as is the extreme pressure that the Archbishop was under during the long captivity of Terry Waite. It was a constant anxiety for him in the midst of all the other demands upon him both from around the Communion and at home.

His extensive travels around the Communion gave him the opportunity to see at first hand the plight of Anglicans and the way some of them bore terrible hardship and suffering. This helped him to put the Church of England into its right perspective. He became convinced that the Church of England had so much to learn from other churches of the Communion. 'We in England ought to be justly proud that we became the mother church of a great Communion. Today we are only one national church within a great partnership'. On another occasion he said to the Anglican Consultative Council, 'I have to spend much time preaching to the Church of England that it is a part of the Anglican Communion.'[11]

The value that Runcie placed upon the personal and relational life of the Anglican Communion was the outworking of his understanding of the nature of the Church as communion, *koinonia*. In line with much ecumenical theology of the time, he saw the Church as the company of those drawn into the life and love of God the Holy Trinity, a life that has to be made visible and credible in this world. The 'glue' that binds the fellowship together is not the juridical, but the personal and relational, always expressed in worship of the Holy Trinity, in the personal sharing of the Eucharist, and in doing something not just with others but for others. 'Communion is not rooted in bonhomie or enjoying one another's company, but in a sense of mutual dependence.'[12] He held that the outworking of *koinonia* could be seen in journeys of support and programmes of partnership. 'I am always glad when I hear of support and programmes of partnership between provinces, schemes that strengthen communion between them.' He sent Bishop Keith Sutton to attend a tragic funeral in South Africa in 1985, and in 1989 a group under the leadership of Archbishop Ted Scott to Namibia at a critical time for the future of that country. It was the gift of *koinonia* that he saw as sustaining the enormous diversity which he came to value so much in his travels around the provinces of the Communion as an expression of the 'generosity and creativity' of God. He believed that the one gospel had to be expressed and lived out relevantly in each cultural context. Preaching at the Mar Thoma Maramon Convention in 1989, in Kerala, he told those Indian Christians in a church in communion with his own church,

> Your continuing loyalty to St Thomas is an important witness to the fact that the Gospel has to be planted in each nation in a way such as to present intact its culture and customs. The Gospel must be at home and in touch with the place and the people where it has taken root.[13]

He applauded the Anglican way, which at its best exhibited an ability to value diversity, for as he wrote 'only a Church which can comprehend diversity can believe in the developing unfolding of God's truth'. 'We could make our Communion much more tidy, but it would be much less loveable, and we should be imprisoned as a result.'

But it was precisely this rich diversity of churches, autonomous and yet interdependent, that raised the sharpest question for him and one that he wrestled with throughout his time as Archbishop. Diversity so often led to difference and became a threat to the very Communion that he so cared about. During his archiepiscopate this was focused in the matter of the ordination of women to the presbyterate and the episcopate, a matter which touched the ordained ministry and thus an essential bond of the Church's unity and communion. Although himself conservative on this issue, indeed he was against the ordination of women when he took up his role as Archbishop, he knew that conflict would always be a part of the life of the Church and that there was a danger in trying to avoid it or any divisive issue. But how was coherence to be maintained, unity safeguarded, when the absolute authority of independent provinces meant that the province was the only place where authoritative decisions could be made? What was the meaning of interdependence when provinces went ahead alone? He was aware that critics accused the Anglican Communion of being 'soggy at the centre', guilty of 'episcopal or diocesan congregationalism'. He himself believed that the shibboleth of provincial independence needed to be scrutinized. Again and again he posed the question of whether the Anglican Communion needed ways and occasions together when decisions could be taken that might be binding on all. He saw the need to strengthen the coherence of the Communion.

Already when he assumed his role as Archbishop an examination was underway on the instruments of Anglican unity: the Lambeth Conference of Bishops, established in 1887, which met every ten years; the Anglican Consultative Council, made up of bishops, clergy and laity from the provinces, established in 1969, which met regularly between Lambeth Conferences; and a Meeting of Primates established in 1978. Runcie recognized that the coming into existence of these different bodies had been attempts to address the question of the coherence of the Communion.

But, by the time Runcie became Archbishop in 1980, their very existence had come to raise questions. Among these questions were: what authority did each possess and should their resolutions be binding on the provinces or not? What was the relation of an episcopal body to a synodical body? What was the role of an Archbishop of Canterbury? And, what should the relationship be between the Secretary General of the Anglican Communion and the Archbishop of Canterbury? How might the different instruments best serve the coherence and unity of the Communion?

Runcie's most sustained thinking about the coherence of the Communion and the role of the different instruments of unity comes in his book *Authority in Crisis?*, the result of an 'Archbishop thinking on his feet' as he described it.[14] He was sure of what he called 'the inevitability of authority' and that to believe in God, the ultimate reality, is to believe in authority. The New Testament points to the authority of God, mediated in Christ and continuing in the mission to the world through the communion of faith. So, the question for him was not whether the Church has authority but of what sort, and how it is to be exercised. He approved the Anglican notion of dispersed authority and the way of appeal to Scripture, Tradition and reason, and saw their strength as in their combination and relation. What was needed was a constant dialogue between Church and gospel with an interplay between reason, culture, experience and once-and-for-all revelation. He believed that the Church will reach a common mind on issues, not easily, nor without controversy, but steadily and surely. What was controverted opinion had to be tested and scrutinized, and either rejected or eventually accepted as part of the continuing tradition of the Church, in continuity with the past and in conformity with Scripture, and yet identical with neither. In this process he saw the essential ministry of the bishop as one of keeping the Church true to the implications of the gospel. He did not consider to be unprovidential either the development of the autonomous provinces, together with the role of the Archbishop of Canterbury, nor the calling of Lambeth Conferences without the promptings of the Spirit. He saw the development of the Anglican Consultative Council and the Primates' Meeting as having responded to particular needs. The institutionalized voice of the laity with the model of bishop-in-synod was important to him, however uncomfortable he might sometimes appear sitting through the debates of the Church of England's General Synod. In the end the dialogue between gospel and Church requires the interplay of the different sources, aspects and levels of authority. The *consensus fidelium* is not about correct procedures or the external credentials of authoritative persons or institutions. It is rather about that complex theological question of how the whole Church 'receives' the decisions of bishops, councils and synods.

> In the end – but not usually quickly – God's Spirit will show the whole Church whether such a decision or development had its origin in the same Spirit or not. There are no short cuts, no easy ways. I speak as a modest historian of the early church.[15]

For all his wrestling with the question of authority and coherence, Runcie seems not, at least in the time before Lambeth 1988, to have taken the step of actually advocating that either a Lambeth Conference or a strengthened Anglican Consultative Council should become a binding authority for all the provinces of the Communion. Certainly it never occurred to him to think that the role of an Archbishop of Canterbury should become papal. On more than one occasion he said that he had no intention of developing an alternative Papacy. He would rather deal with the existing one and help in its reform as a ministry for all. This was a consequence of his view of the provisionality of the Anglican Communion. His convictions were more than simply the result of his assessment that the Provinces would never accept such developments. It was his firm conviction that, however painful, decision-making on controversial issues in such a diverse communion takes time, involves different sources and instruments and, because of the provisional nature of the Anglican Communion, requires consultation with other Christians. This middle way did not satisfy either those in the Communion who believed in naked autonomy for provinces, nor those who looked for a more centralized, solid and authoritarian form of government. He was accused of being weak and of sitting on the fence. But, partly as a result of his own constant questioning and examination of the structures, he did make them work and relate to each other. This was strengthened by a close working relationship with the Secretary General of the Anglican Consultative Council.

It was in his steering of the Communion on the matter of the ordination of women to the episcopate, although he probably did not realize it at the time, that his understanding of decision-making in the Communion of Anglican Churches was put into practice and is in fact still being tested. Runcie knew that this matter of unity ought not to be decided definitively by a single province, nor indeed by the Anglican Communion. He called for a Working Party, under the chairmanship of John Grindrod, Archbishop of Brisbane in Australia, to review the way in which the different provinces in their different cultural contexts saw the matter, as well as how ecumenical partners were handling the same issue.[16] He asked for the theological arguments for and against to be clearly set out for the bishops coming to the Lambeth Conference. He himself actively guided the planning of the Conference presentations to the bishops, ensuring that all opinions were presented and that the voice of women, including ordained women, should be heard and that the voice of ecumenical partners, including the Orthodox and Roman Catholic churches, should not be excluded. He was adamant that sufficient time should be given to consideration of the matter. In line with his own thinking and writing in advance on the matter, he knew that a final answer could not be given for all time. In fact the Conference did open the way for provinces, now with the approval of the Lambeth Conference, to take a decision, and for other provinces to remain in the 'highest possible degree of communion' with those from whom they differed. The Conference opened the way for the matter to be seen in that on-going process of discernment that Runcie had written about in his book on authority. After the Conference he insisted that that ongoing process be followed carefully and monitored by the commission he set up under the chairmanship of Robin Eames, Archbishop of Armagh. As Runcie said:

If a thing is of God it will flourish – if not it will eventually
wither. In the meantime we have to endure the pain felt by
protagonists and antagonists alike – that is the cost of dialogue
between Church and Gospel.[17]

But even after the Lambeth Conference, Runcie, characteristically, continued to wrestle with the question of the coherence
of the Communion and how decisions should be made. In
addressing the Anglican Consultative Council in 1990 he
returned to the tension between two forms of authority, baptis-
mal and ministerial.

> We ought to have the courage to allow both the Anglican
> Consultative Council and the Lambeth Conference to assume
> a synodical role when particular need arises. A resolution
> agreed by both bodies might then be accepted by the Com-
> munion as a whole, but by common assent, rather than the
> rule of law. That would also do something to unite those two
> streams of inherent authority . . .
>
>   Why should not the Lambeth Conference, the Anglican
> Consultative Council or the Primates' Meeting be more flex-
> ible for what is required for the particular occasion – even an
> authoritative decision of faith or order for the whole Com-
> munion?[18]

Here Runcie seemed to be moving further in the direction of
centralized, binding authority than in his earlier writing. But
even here he takes care to admit that councils may still err. No
matter how representative a body may be, its decisions may be
mistaken. In the end the whole Church, and by this he does not
only mean the Anglican Communion, has to receive the decisions
of popes, bishops, councils and synods. And this can never be
reduced to a legal process. In acceptance or rejection, in modifi-
cation or development, the whole people of God has an essential
and decisive part to play. Here is the ultimate assurance of truth
in the Church: the gift of the Holy Spirit in baptism to the whole
body of Christ. In the end Runcie knew that to believe in some
perfect system of Church government is to succumb to a fantasy,

to a dream which hinders the healing of the gospel. Nevertheless, he did believe, with some modesty that,

> our [Anglican] recipe may have something to be said for it, as all the churches come together ... traditional authoritarianism, the more recent permissive liberal free-for-all, and the inevitable lurch back into neo-conservatism ... [are] all mistaken ways of looking at authority ... [19]

It is too soon to give any definitive assessment of Robert Runcie's contribution to the Anglican Communion. In some ways his legacy on coherence and staying in communion is still being tested in the ongoing reception of the matter of the ordination of women. But it can be seen that by his own theological wrestling with the issues of authority and decision-making and his guiding of the Communion in response to the issue of women's ordination, he offered a credible, dynamic and flexible way of discernment in communion. He ensured that the provisionality of the Anglican Communion was never forgotten, that its diversity was affirmed and that it was kept open to all our ecumenical partners. He could not escape the task of wrestling with the matter of Anglican coherence but he knew very well that there were far more urgent needs facing humankind and that it was important that we show that we believe that Christ and the gospel can make a difference to that world. We are the bearers of God's promise to save and renew humanity. The picture of communion that Anglicans show is a way that they indicate that we are bearers of the good news, and can help to restore individuals and societies to peace and health. Our commitment to world mission will be more specific and focused if we have an understanding of the resources, the character and the particular vocation of the Anglican Communion. Anglican communion and unity, and Christian unity and communion were important as signs and instruments of human unity.

Of his own role in the Anglican Communion he always spoke with modesty. He knew there was always pressure on him to make snap judgements, to speak on behalf of his own and every province. The media found it easier to focus on a single figure and he knew the dangers of this. He was the senior bishop of the Communion, but I am, 'still one bishop among many', my role is 'fraternal and not papal ... to gather the Churches, not to rule them ... sometimes to speak for it'. He saw an Archbishop of Canterbury's task as a representative focus for unity, not for the sake of some monolithic international structure, but for the sake of rich diversity. He jokingly referred to the time that he was described as 'Lord High Primate', which sounds he said like a monkey in a treetop!

The sense of what living in communion means was heightened in the 'affective communion' he offered by way of friendship and identification with others, especially those parts of the Communion that suffered. The impact he made on those he met was summed up in the tributes from around the Communion that were given at the Anglican Consultative Council in 1990. Bishop Sumio Takatsu of Brazil recalled Runcie's visit to Brazil and how the Roman Catholic Archbishop of Sao Paulo had described him as 'a messenger of God, an apostle of peace, a friend of the poor and defender of human rights'. Archbishop Robinson of Australia added that no visiting Archbishop of Canterbury had ever endeared himself so quickly to the Church of Australia as Robert Runcie. Bishop David Gitari, from Tanzania, talked of the encouragement the Archbishop had given him personally and Bishop James Ottley from the Caribbean claimed that he had made the office of Archbishop of Canterbury become real and alive for his people. But no one summed up better his gift for making friends and building relationships around the Communion than the Presiding Bishop of the Episcopal Church in the USA. He recalled a visit Runcie had made to Hawaii. It was at the time of an outbreak of hepatitis and people tried to persuade the Archbishop not to go on walkabout or to get too close to people. But instead, the Archbishop went into a simple home and sat down next to a small figure huddled on a bench. 'I'm Robert,' he said, 'what's your name?'

6. Friendship Before Theology: Runcie and the Churches

CHRISTOPHER HILL

No obituary of Robert Runcie failed to mention his praying together with Pope John Paul II in Canterbury Cathedral in May 1982. That icon of prayer at the Martyrdom in the Cathedral is etched on many memories. But Runcie was the last person to cherish an exclusive ecumenism. Because he believed in catholic Christianity his ecumenism was universal. Its wellsprings were more personal than theological, more historical than institutional.

Robert's father was a non-practising Presbyterian Scot. In Liverpool – Great Crosby – the Runcie family asked Robert's father, at the time of the Church of England–Church of Scotland conversations in the 1950s, why he was getting so upset about the proposal that bishops be adopted in the Kirk. 'We thought you were an atheist, Dad': 'Aye,' came the answer, 'but I'm a Presbyterian atheist'. In spite of learning the faith, or better praying the faith, at the Anglo-Catholic St Faith's, Great Crosby, Robert retained a familial respect for the Reformed tradition, even if its drier spirituality had little emotional appeal.

Later in life, through a family marriage, Robert was also to know something of the opportunities and pains of an Anglican–Roman Catholic marriage. It has been said, rightly, that he in many ways retained a 'lay' view of life. Certainly he was close to lay Roman Catholic commitment which did not always express itself in the ways of clerical conformity.

At university one of his teachers was the great Methodist historian and theologian Gordon Rupp. Whenever Robert encountered Methodists he acknowledged his debt to this great scholar. He also sustained continuing friendships with Methodist leaders and theologians such as the late Gordon Wakefield.

The war widened human and ecclesiastical horizons. With advance into Europe Robert came to know a Dutch family, and from this emerged a long friendship and occasional correspondence with Jo van Beeck, Fr Jo van Beeck SJ, Cody Professor of Theology in Chicago, another friend at the more radical end of the Roman Catholic spectrum.

Immediately after the war Robert returned to Oxford, only to become one of the first exchange students between Oxford and Bonn. Apart from fraternization with a soprano from the Cologne Opera, Robert there first came into contact with the theological convictions of German Catholicism and Protestantism. Though this contact was not profound, his antennae sensed something of the varied cultural roots of Western European Christianity. The Church of England was not centre stage after all.

His visits to India both before and during his sojourn at Canterbury pushed even further back his mental frontiers. Friendship with Nadir Dinshaw reinforced this, just as friendship with Rabbi Dan Cohn-Sherbok allowed him profound insights into the Jewish community and its remembrance of the Holocaust.

His first contacts with the Orthodox were more literary, though they did not lack elements of personal friendship. It was Robert's love of the classical world which fired his interest in those who were in some ways the successors of the Hellenistic world: the Orthodox Churches. Byzantine history, rather than theology, were congenial to Robert. He loved the cultural rootedness of the Orthodox, comparing this unfavourably with much deracinated and ephemeral experience in the Christian West.

It was, therefore, with the Orthodox internationally and the Roman Catholics locally that Runcie was best known ecumenically on the eve of his enthronement in Canterbury. Michael Ramsey recognized his interest in all things Byzantine and knew that there was nothing so Byzantine as what was then called the Anglican–Orthodox Joint Doctrinal Discussions, of which he appointed Runcie Anglican Co-Chairman. In spite of good theological agreements the Orthodox, by 1982, had rumbled that Anglicans were not simply, or not at all, an innocent survival of Celtic, non-Roman, episcopal Christianity: a Western Orthodoxy allied in Byzantine manner to the great British Empire by the British Sovereign. It was the ordination of women and the statements of liberal bishops which disabused the Orthodox. Anglicans had the Reformation and the Enlightenment in their bloodstream, as well as a more ancient Celtic and Roman foundation.

Robert once described an Anglican–Orthodox meeting at which the Secretary General of the Anglican Communion had been invited to denounce, or at least cover up, the ordination of women. Bishop John Howe duly listed province after province of the Anglican Communion which were contemplating or which had ordained women to the diaconate and presbyterate, and which might potentially ordain to the episcopate. The veil had been lifted.

It was one of Robert Runcie's greatest achievements that the conversations were not ended more or less permanently there and then. Following this meeting he spent a calculated sabbatical touring the Orthodox Churches of the Mediterranean, Near East, the Balkans and Russia. Robert had learnt diplomacy by secondment at the end of the war to the Trieste Boundary Commission. These skills were to come to the fore in his being able to return from his sabbatical with commitment to continuing dialogue with the Orthodox in the bag in spite of the ordination of women.

He also returned with some wonderful stories. The Patriarch of Antioch had received him cheerfully, in spite of being hours late as taxi drivers in Antioch are not quite so well trained as those in London. They agreed on the need for charity and continued conversation. But on leaving, the Patriarch warned Robert about the danger of theology: charity unites, theology divides was his parting shot! Runcie, who was rather suspicious of overmuch theology, tacitly agreed. Runcie came to Orthodoxy – and to other traditions as well – through friendship, rather than dialogue. Long before he had come to know the old Bishop Josef of Rimnic, in the Carpathian foothills of Romania, through his son Lucian Gafton who was at Cuddesdon under Runcie, as an ecumenical student.

At home he hugely enjoyed the company and intellectual

stimulation of the late Bishop Christopher Butler, Auxiliary Bishop of Westminster in Hertfordshire, who was enthroned in a loaned St Alban's Abbey. Joint eucharistic reservation in the (Local Ecumenical Project) joint church at Pin Green was, however, always alleged by Robert to have been accepted at a meeting at which Christopher Butler had momentarily dozed off. Robert Runcie relished Christopher Butler's company and sharp mind, whether discussing the implications of the Second Vatican Council, which Butler attended as Abbot of Downside, or the origin and dating of the Gospels, a matter on which Butler had once written but was always open to fresh argument.

On arrival at Lambeth therefore Robert Runcie knew that he was known for ecumenism in a certain direction. One of his first ecumenical questions was how to address this strategically and how and by whom the 'foreign policy' of the Church of England was determined. In 1980 the Church of England's ecumenical staff resources were curiously dispersed. The Board for Mission and Unity of the General Synod was largely in practice and agenda concerned with more domestic ecumenical relations in this country – inheriting something of an earlier division between its predecessor the Missionary and Ecumenical Council and the Church of England Council on Foreign Relations. The latter, shorn of its council, was based at Lambeth and had become the Archbishops' Counsellors on Foreign Relations. This office also then largely staffed international Anglican dialogues such as the Roman Catholic, Orthodox and Lutheran on behalf of the Anglican Communion. To complicate matters the Free Churches (and interfaith contacts) were handled at Lambeth by another department. Runcie's question had been apt. The answer, after a report by Bishop Graham Leonard, then of Truro, led eventually to some significant changes, not all for the good in terms of staff levels, with the Lambeth ecumenical staff becoming more personal to the Archbishop but also more interconnected with General Synod and Anglican Communion ecumenical departments. Structures were not Runcie's thing, however, and there is still a task to be completed. A significant change for good was the heightened European profile of the General Synod.

Later at Lambeth Robert was to speak of 'all round' and 'all level' ecumenism. Even before speaking in these terms he wanted to signal his inclusive vision and commitment. How could he do this in a recognizable way? The answer to Robert's question about his ecumenical profile came from Martin Luther, whose five-hundredth anniversary of birth fell in 1983. Once it became known that the Archbishop of Canterbury would personally welcome an invitation to the Luther celebrations in both (as it was) East and West Germany the stage was set for a strategic archiepiscopal thrust with a major European Church. His proleptic German exchange after the war, not to speak (and he rarely did) of his actual war record in Germany, now became background for a major ecumenical visit. Something of the circumstances of his Military Cross had leaked out: he had single-handedly knocked out a German tank. But there was German respect for a real soldier, indeed a *Panzer Commandant*. In major speeches and sermons, often quoting the more positive affirmations about the continental Protestant Churches by the Caroline Divines, and by availing himself of an Anglican liberty to communicate on special occasions, Robert's visit became a major stimulus for the Meissen Conversations and the Agreement which followed. In particular his liberality rejoiced in some famous words of Bishop Lancelot Andrewes specifically addressed to the Continental Protestant Churches on the subject of bishops:

> But even if our order be admitted to be of divine authority, it does not follow that without it there can be no salvation, or that without it a Church cannot stand. Only a blind man could fail to see Churches standing without it. Only a man of iron could deny that salvation is to be found within them. We are not men of iron . . .[1]

After keeping the Orthodox on hold, Runcie had actually connected with the German Lutherans and Reformed (the Evangelische Kirche in Deutschland having Lutheran, Reformed and Union member Churches). The Porvoo Agreement with the Nordic and Baltic Churches developed in its turn from the stimulus of the Meissen Agreement building on earlier agreements with those churches.

Less obvious was Robert Runcie's support for the Coven-
anting Proposals between the Church of England, the Methodist
Church, the URC and the Moravians of 1982. His speech to
General Synod, though in favour, probably damned the scheme
with faint praise. The Covenant was a prelude to full unity but
would have considerably increased ecumenical bureaucracy and
ecclesiastical meetings. Nor was he convinced that there had
been a thorough enough agreement to warrant the reconciliation
of ministries proposed in the Covenant.

At gatherings of the British Council of Churches he was
conspicuous for his commitment and stamina rather than his
enjoyment of the corporate culture of Free Church assemblies,
of which the BCC was an example. But nor did he care for
General Synod and its committees. Though Runcie's presidency
of the British Council of Churches was not a thing he found
naturally easy, his role, always exercised with modesty and self-
depreciation, was appreciated more than he realized. Through
the British Council of Churches he also gained some experience
of the smaller churches in Britain and Ireland. An Assembly
at Llandudno was personally memorable for him because his
grandmother took him there on holiday from Liverpool. He
rejoiced in the nuances of the different churches of Wales. On
national occasions he was always concerned to include the other
churches fully, in spite of his continuing belief in establishment.
He came to speak for all at the Falklands Service in St Paul's
Cathedral to such effect that a distinguished Free Church person
was heard to say (at a time when Robert was being strongly
criticized by Government and internally in the Church of England): 'If the Anglicans don't want Bob Runcie as their Archbishop, we will be happy to have him as ours!'

On a global scale Runcie was similarly ambivalent in his participation in the Vancouver Assembly of the World Council of
Churches in 1983. It was a duty rather than a joy, with huge
questions about representation and ecclesiastical democracy.
The over-directive, issue-focused and at times manipulative
directorate gave Runcie many qualms. But he loved meeting the
delegates. His staff were sent on foraging parties for samosas
and wine so that the Archbishop could give some hospitality to
Christians from all over the world and from every Christian

Church. And occasionally to bolster up a little bit of revolt in the Assembly, to rouse support for a beleaguered Faith and Order Commission, or to actually meet fellow Anglicans – provision for which had been originally excluded by design. Most successful of all was the Vancouver Worship Tent. Different spiritual traditions worshipped with their own integrity. A final Eucharist, at which he presided, raised some Anglo-Catholic eyebrows at home. As in Germany he advanced ecumenically by gesture and prayer rather than through constitutions and schemes. He enjoyed the presence of a Danish woman priest alongside him at the altar at that final Eucharist: and was impressed by her rigorous theological training. Once again friendship counted more than theology and he rejoiced to celebrate the Eucharist flanked not only by a Danish Lutheran woman pastor but a Reformed from Indonesia, a Methodist from Benin, a Baptist from Hungary, a Moravian from Jamaica and a minister of the United Church of Canada. That indeed was 'all round' ecumenism, with Orthodox and Roman Catholic priests also present but not communicating.

Robert spoke of 'all levels' as well as 'all round'. After the failure of the Covenant Proposals he gave solid support to the drafting of the ecumenical canons (B43 and B44). What was not yet possible internationally, or nationally, became possible in a committed relationship locally. For the first time the Church of England gave official recognition of an ordained ministry and the reality of Word and Sacrament in other churches. This local canonical provision also made possible the later agreements with the German and French Protestant churches. Robert's own personal experience of Local Ecumenical Projects as Bishop of St Albans resulted in his fullest support for these genuinely radical (though very carefully worded) canons.

Of course not everything was an ecumenical success. His most spectacular and notorious ecumenical failure, on his own admission, was at a World Council of Churches Conference on the Community of Women and Men at Sheffield in 1981. Robert was nervous about the occasion, an international gathering of (largely) women theologians. He received briefings and suggested lines for his address from his own staff and from Church House. He also asked another woman theologian (or rather, congenially, an academic historian) for her thoughts. These included examples of how not to create a community of women and men, including an offensive quotation from Martin Luther about women. The dead-pan, play-this-with-a-straight-bat advice from staff was set aside and Robert risked English self-deprecating humour with an audience largely composed of women for whom English was a second or third language. Disaster and real anger resulted. Some certainly thought he was quoting Luther favourably. Robert was always honest and gracious. He apologized to staff teams afterwards and was thereafter cautious about high-table humour in argument with those of a different cultural background. The Sheffield visit was only redeemed, on the feminine front, by a breakfast meeting the following morning with the Lord Mayor of Sheffield who happened to be Roy Hattersley's redoubtable mother!

And Rome? Robert had, as I have already noted, a number of lay and radical Roman Catholic friends. This did not mean he despised Rome as an ecclesiastical institution, still less the Papacy. Nevertheless, if he was asked what impressed him most about the Roman Catholic Church his answer was the devotion and commitment of its religious communities, both formal and informal, which he saw on his many travels all over the world. And also its commitment to inculturation, much in advance of most provinces of the Anglican Communion. Perhaps it was this freedom to set aside European trappings in a universal communion which led him to respect the ministry of the Bishop of Rome as an instrument of universal communion. Certainly more than once he encouraged Anglican churches to take on the face of their culture in the confidence that Anglicanism did not imply Englishness, and he materially developed the role of the See of Canterbury as an instrument of wider communion without cultural imperialism. Robert Runcie was able to speak positively about ecumenical recognition of a Roman Primacy because his own office was in a lesser sense also a Petrine ministry of unity.

Robert Runcie met Pope John Paul II no less than five times in ten years, the first being in Accra, Ghana. The late Cardinal Basil Hume, on being told by telephone that this was being arranged, misheard the venue as 'a car'! It was in the Papal

Nuncio's house rather than a car that Runcie invited the Pope to Canterbury. There was a genuine rapport between the Polish Pope and the Liverpool–Oxbridge Archbishop. Conversation was never vibrant, Robert's delivery was always slow with the Pope, probably wisely in view of his own English drawl and occasionally recondite vocabulary. But there seemed to be a mutual understanding. On their last meeting in Rome, after an excellent lunch together, the Pope spoke of there being an 'affective collegiality' between Anglicans and Roman Catholics which must become (one day) 'effective collegiality'. Threat? Promise? Certainly an interesting ecclesiological development.

Assessments of the Papal Visit to England, and especially to Canterbury, differ. In contrasting obituaries, David Edwards spoke of potential and promise unfulfilled; Andrew Brown, interestingly, was more positive:

> The Pope's visit to Canterbury in 1982 was postponed by the Falklands War. But when it came, it was as close as we may ever get to a Roman Catholic recognition of the Church of England as a real, Catholic church. It may have marked a profound change in English self-understanding: English patriotism has long been entwined with anti-Catholicism ... Runcie's gracious, generous and intelligent handling of these matters was hugely important in showing that attitudes had changed, as well as in changing them.[2]

It was in Canterbury that Runcie suggested to the Pope his hopes for some event of prayer for world peace for all the communities of faith. Robert believed that only the Pope could issue such an invitation credibly. Some time later Pope John Paul II invited world religious leaders to Assisi for a Day of Prayer. Whether this was a direct result of Robert's suggestion, or whether the Pope was thinking similarly, we may never know. Interestingly the Day of Prayer was given live television coverage all over the world, comparable to the Olympics, except in Britain.

Alongside more public events there continued the patient work of the Anglican Roman Catholic International Commission (ARCIC) dialogue. Equally there also developed a momentum towards the ordination of women. Once again

Runcie the diplomat ensured continuing dialogue alongside the problems raised by such a new obstacle to unity – as the ordination of women was perceived to be by Rome. Though in favour theologically Runcie as Archbishop opposed the ordination of women to the priesthood (he supported entry to the diaconate) on grounds of ecumenical and internal Anglican unity. But he knew its time would come. In 1985 he wrote a very carefully drafted letter to Cardinal Willebrands stating succinctly what was in his view the major reason for the ordination of women to the presbyterate on grounds of patristic and catholic theology. It was firm but not antagonistic. Runcie's central argument was based on the rock-like foundation of the patristic affirmation that 'what is not assumed is not healed (saved)'. In other words the incarnation is about the whole of humanity – male and female – being taken into the Godhead through the Incarnation. If only male humanity is assumed only males can be saved. Thus the humanity which we celebrate as in God in the ascension of the Lord must be potentially all humanity. As well as the whole people of God being priestly, there is also a representative priestly role in the ordained ministry. And the High Priesthood of Christ that the priest represents in presiding at the Eucharist must therefore potentially include all humanity. It is therefore fully appropriate that women are ordained to the priesthood. It is a patristic and catholic argument for the inclusion of women in the priesthood, an inclusion which Runcie saw as an authentic development of the ordained ministry rather than its over-turning. To this day there has not been an open and official dialogue with Rome about the theological reasons for and against the ordination of women. But the fact that the dialogue continues at all owes much to Robert Runcie's commitment to reconciliation and unity.

Robert Runcie followed the ARCIC dialogue closely, both through staff and his longstanding personal friendship with Mark Santer, Bishop of Birmingham and Anglican Co-Chairman of the conversations. But once again he was less concerned with theology than people and friendship. His final meeting, as Archbishop, with the Pope took place in Rome in 1989. He allowed his sense of history to complement ARCIC's theology of a universal primacy (rather than supremacy) of the Bishop of

Rome. So he put on the agenda, in official speeches in Rome and back home in the General Synod, the idea of an Anglican (and wider) acceptance of the 'primacy of charity' in Rome recognized by the fathers and still today by the Orthodox. Though this was (relatively) obvious to anybody with a sense of the history of the whole Church, it was a courageous thing to do and it caused re-echoed cries of 'Runcie the Romanizer' from Paisleyite quarters and among some in the Church of England.

To have advanced the Church of England ecumenically with the German churches may have been a surprise to Robert himself. It was, however, the real achievement of his 'Luther' visits. Only he could have kept the Orthodox dialogue going at its most troubled time. Robert Runcie also barred the way back to 'No Popery' in his invitation to John Paul II to visit Canterbury, and also began to speak about a Roman Primacy for the sake of unity, which was a major stimulus for Pope John Paul's own ecumenical invitation to reflect on that Primacy in his Papal Encyclical *Ut Unum Sint* (1995).

There was a personal cost to Robert Runcie's ecumenical commitment. Although he did not gladly suffer fools he could be enormously patient with those he disagreed with. On a visit to the Coptic Orthodox Church in Egypt, Robert endured a whole morning's lecture, from Genesis to Revelation, on why women should not be ordained from Pope Shenouda himself. His only remark afterwards was that the Coptic Pope had been using a King James version of the English Bible which he knew the Pope had read from cover to cover during long house arrest in earlier troubled times between Muslim extremists and Christians in Egypt. It was a Bible of the kind which had coloured type for the words of God and Jesus. More difficult was a moment during the visit of the Oecumenical Patriarch of Constantinople, primus-inter-pares of all the Orthodox churches. The party were in Canterbury at the Old Palace and had just retired to bed when Robert had an urgent telephone call from Lambeth. The Principal of Pusey House was on the telephone to Lambeth. Dr Gary Bennett, an Oxford church historian of some distinction, had committed suicide. Dr Bennett was the 'anonymous' author of the Preface to *Crockford's Clerical*

Directory. The Preface had criticized Robert's 'liberalism' so unmistakably that it was not difficult to recognize its authorship. Gary Bennett was an old friend. The following day the programme with the Oecumenical Patriarch continued and it was only afterwards that the Orthodox party learned of the tragedy and the personal strain that the Archbishop of Canterbury had endured during the remaining days of their programme in London.

Robert Runcie's ecumenical vision was always wider than the institutional churches. In his opening address to the Lambeth Conference 1988 Robert Runcie made this clear to an Anglican Communion also in need of a ministry of unity. In this major address Runcie moved from unity within the Anglican Communion, through unity among all the Christian churches towards the unity of all human communities and all creation: the unity of the Kingdom. The address was not a dry systematic exercise. It was punctuated throughout by stories of people he had met and learned from. Friendship, as ever, spiced his theology. He began with the book of Revelation (21.22–27) and its statement that 'the gates of the City shall not be shut'. As he put it: 'Exclusiveness is not a characteristic of the City of God.' He ended with Ephesians (1.9–10):

> For (God) has made known to us in all wisdom and insight the mystery of his will, according to his purpose which he set forth in Christ as a plan for the fullness of time, to unite all things in him, things in heaven and things on earth.

His rejection of exclusiveness and his embrace of the *pleroma* of Ephesians is for me a characteristic and fitting epitaph for the one hundred and second Archbishop of Canterbury.

It was never a sinecure to work for Robert Runcie: it was a privilege which leaves me with lasting affection for him.

7. Pastoral Pragmatist: Runcie as Communicator

RICHARD HARRIES

John Drury, the Dean of Christ Church, Oxford, says that when Bob Runcie was Dean of Trinity Hall he was a very popular figure and 'He liked to be so'. He tells the story of an incident after a grand feast at Trinity Hall.

> We were in the Master's drawing room and Bob beckoned to me and my undergraduate friends saying, 'John, Joel and Anthony do come over here and gather round me. I want to look popular because the Archbishop's patronage secretary is here tonight'.

It was a characteristic mixture of self-promotion and self-deprecation, sincerity and irony. The main thing about Bob was his universal human appeal.

John Drury goes on to refer to the Dean's evenings of lively, intellectual conversation with a range of speakers and his devoted pastoral care both of undergraduates and dons. In private conversation John Drury remembers the devotional feel of his sermons in College Chapel. The word it is important to note in that memory is 'devotional'. While allowing for a change in preaching styles generally from that time and a change in Runcie's own approach, particularly when faced with less intimate audiences, what is signified by that word remained the bedrock of his sermons and lectures on Christian themes. When he died the *Daily Telegraph* editorial referred to his 'humorous, unsaintly way' and Clifford Longley in the same newspaper wrote that 'He had little malice but was not a great saint'. One is tempted to reply – how does he know? It might be thought that Runcie was a worldly man. So he was: in the same way that Jesus was (Matthew 11.19). After his death someone that knew him well wrote to Mother Rosemary of the Sisters of the Love of God at Fairacres in Oxford to say:

> Jeremy Taylor once said, 'Lord, give us affable souls' but I think Robert's unfailing affability has concealed from too many the rocklike attendance to God and duty that was his daily bread throughout this time.

I was at Cuddesdon from 1961 to 1963, not long after Robert Runcie had taken over as Principal. The contrast in preaching styles of members of staff at the time is instructive in bringing out Robert Runcie's particular strengths. There was John Ruston, deeply devout, Peter Cornwall engaging with the social and political issues of the time, Lionel Wickham somehow combining high theology and levity, and Anthony Bird, far from fluent but deeply serious. Runcie's sermons stand out from the others with their sense of being carefully crafted and gently persuasive of Christian orthodoxy. The description of his sermons as carefully crafted is a point I would want to emphasize at the outset. There are those who think that Runcie's sometimes superb sentences came spontaneously. On the whole they didn't. They were the result of serious intellectual engagement with what he wanted to say and how it could be best said. A form of communication which could make those of us who heard it at the time want mentally to clap our hands were his introductions to visiting speakers. In a very few sentences there would be a vignette of the person about to give the talk, replete with affectionate humour, together with an indication of why what they were about to say was important. However, if you went to the loo a few minutes before such a lecture you would have seen the Principal pacing the corridor working the words of his few well-chosen sentences together in his mind. Of course there was a natural talent, and he could speak in a masterly fashion on some occasions without such preparation: but these moments were made possible by all the sheer hard work that had gone in on so many similar occasions before.

The high point of study at Cuddesdon at that time (perhaps it still is) was the principal's (known as Princeps) lectures on prayer. Rereading my notes of the lectures after nearly 40 years they are as apt now as they were then. They are of course well constructed, with many arresting quotations. But what stands out above all is their realism and practicality. It is sometimes useful to ask about a sermon: is it interesting? Is it helpful? Is it true? For a sermon can be interesting without being helpful or true. Runcie was almost invariably interesting in what he had to say. What comes across in these lectures is his desire to be helpful. It is also noteworthy how biblically based they are, with nearly every point being supported by appropriate passages from the Bible. Not surprisingly they draw on the long tradition of Christian teaching on prayer, with evidence of wide reading. They are also traditional. It was a time when Harry Williams was encouraging people to be more accepting of themselves, less riddled with guilt. Runcie argues for taking sin seriously, with many of his characteristic touches. Highlighting Calvary as God's answer to sin he said, 'To the Greeks foolishness, to the Jews a stumbling block, to the Englishman a perpetual source of embarrassment'. If these had been lectures in a philosophy of religion course then the questions would have been sharper and the probing deeper. But they weren't. They were lectures by a priest to those training for the priesthood. As such they provided the best context for Robert Runcie's strengths. Difficulties were acknowledged, not explored. They were to be lived with on the basis of a gospel faith.

Robert Runcie's time as Bishop of St Albans was one of the happiest periods of his ministry. What comes out from his time as a diocesan bishop in St Albans and later when he acted as a diocesan within the See of Canterbury was his very direct personal communication with the clergy (as well as people he knew who were in need) through letters and telephone calls. Malcolm Lesiter, later Archdeacon of Bedford, has written to say, 'As a parish priest at the time, the main means of communication was by letter and handwritten note.' I have seen the letter Bob Runcie wrote to Malcolm on 29 January 1973 asking him to consider going to the parish of Leavesden. It is thoughtful, prayerful, honest about the parish and appropriately cajoling: 'I must put into Leavesden a man who is firm but flexible. I reckon that this might be you and it would be someone who had a deal of respect from others in the diocese.' It even ends up with a carrot: 'Perhaps I will dangle the possibility of a curate before you if you could go before the ordination season!' The tone is at once serious and light-hearted. It would have been one among scores of letters he would have written every day but it has the unmistakable stamp of a particular person writing to another particular person with a particular aim in view. The other letter from Malcolm Lesiter I have seen is about a difficult pastoral situation which, again, is very much a personal communication, candid, humorous, realistic and characterized by pastoral pragmatism. There is a sense in the letter of the writer and the recipient being on the same side, slightly conspiratorial, amused and both trying to do some good in a wicked world. Malcolm writes:

> I have a useful file of letters and hand written cards which I treasure, not least because he never let his parish clergy feel either forgotten or undervalued . . . It is worth adding that he used to telephone a great deal in communicating with his clergy (usually around 6.oopm) and the clergy knew they had good access to him through his chaplains.

The same characteristics were exhibited during his time as Archbishop in relation to his diocesan work. Bob Hardy, later Bishop of Lincoln but at that time Bishop of Maidstone, has written to say:

> When he was doing a pastoral visit to a parish in my area in the Canterbury Diocese, he would often ring up for some background and I would prepare a briefing paper, both about the parish and about the clergy and ministerial staff. Robert was very acute in using this in a constructive way, and often beefed up my comments and made them much sharper than I had set them out.

Someone also ought to draw attention to the very personal ministry he conducted alongside the burdens of his office. For example, the matron of the hospice in Canterbury developed cancer, and Robert wrote her a couple of marvellous pastoral letters, full of love and wisdom, as she was dying. When I was mauled in the General Synod for the report on *A Way Ahead* Robert sent me a splendid postcard which had a picture of the Second World War poster 'Dig on for Victory'. Robert wrote,

> I ought to have written immediately to commiserate with you over the treatment of your report, cast out by a clever sentence of David Edwards – 'Liberals must not be illiberal'. It is a very sensible report – much more than ours, which I think now did damage, though some good as well. You seem destined to take on adversaries who are too well dug in, hence this card. I hope you and I are as cheerful. Yours ever, Robert.

When it comes to Robert Runcie's national role as Archbishop of Canterbury it is necessary to face at the outset the fact that he used others to write the first draft of his sermons, speeches and lectures. It is well known and now, if not before, readily acknowledged that he made use of a wide range of friends and scholars to write for him. Michael Ramsey, the former Archbishop of Canterbury, apparently said, 'I have never said anything in a speech which I didn't write myself'. But, for a variety of reasons the number of speaking engagements accepted by Runcie was far more than when Ramsey was Archbishop. He could not have responded to these without a very great deal of help. What is unusual is the extent of the help and the form it took. One way of getting help would be to think the main lines of what one wanted to say and then ask someone to write it up with appropriate historical or contextual backing. Or it might be possible to ask someone to do some basic research which one would then integrate into a sermon or lecture. But Runcie used to ring someone up – he himself rang them, not his chaplain, and they were of course appropriately flattered – and they were expected to provide a script as it might actually be delivered. Sometimes he did not use a word of what the person produced. I remember this happening with a script I wrote for him in connection with a service for the fiftieth anniversary of the BBC. One listened in vain for even an echo of what one had so carefully prepared. At other times he used a text virtually unaltered, as he did an article I wrote for him in defence of the British action over the Falklands, which appeared under his name in *The Times*. As Humphrey Carpenter commented

> It was a stiffly phrased article, with none of Runcie's charac-
> teristic touches, as it was almost entirely the work of Richard
> Harries ... the draft which he sent to Runcie on 5th May
> was scarcely altered before publication.

These are extreme examples, however. His most characteristic method was to take the script he had been sent and then work and work on it to make it his own. Graham James, who was Runcie's chaplain from 1987 to 1993, has written:

> The important thing is to recognise how many drafts of these
> sermons went into the Archbishop for his criticism, comment,
> questioning and improvement. He was a critic of the very
> highest order, and that meant that you produced your best
> work for him. It was nothing like being a civil servant produ-
> cing a routine speech for a minister who might glance at it a
> few minutes beforehand. Each of these addresses was pored
> over and he knew them inside out before he preached them.
> That was why they were so convincingly his own, even if he
> had not composed them.

Robert Runcie published two collections of sermons, *One Light for One World*[1] in 1988 and *The Unity We Seek*[2] in 1989. The latter gives a range of addresses from one year during his archiepiscopate. It includes a number of communications for the 1988 Lambeth Conference as well as major addresses on the environment, for conferences of Evangelicals, pilgrims at Glastonbury, to the Russian Orthodox Church and the Jewish community. There is sensitivity and substance in all of them as well as his characteristic knack of coming up with fresh quota-tions. The title is rather dull but it goes wider than simply holding the Anglican Communion together. He addresses evan-gelicals on the importance of biblical scholarship and biblical scholars on the importance of holding their scholarship with faith. The unity he sought was not just ecclesial unity but that profounder unity which unites the honest, enquiring mind and

Christian devotion. *One Light for One World* contains more personal sermons, including one on 'Why I Believe'. This reveals his reluctance to give neat answers to the question. God is ultimate mystery and we deny that mystery, namely, God himself, by neat formulae, whether philosophical or religious. What he could do he thought was 'Point to space for such belief – intellectual, moral and emotional space.' There are deeply felt sermons in relation to Jews, the bombing of Dresden and suffering in general which he regards as the problem facing religious believers at the level of intellect and faith. In a sermon on the Zeebrugge tragedy he spoke words which he used on other occasions as well.

> Christian faith does not mean believing in impossible things. It means trusting that Christ's promises never fail ... Faith is not hoping the worst won't happen. It is knowing there is no tragedy which cannot be redeemed.[3]

As might be expected he is particularly good on historical figures such as Lord Shaftesbury, St Hugh, T. S. Eliot and John Bunyan. In the foreword to this collection he acknowledged the help he received from other scriptwriters and justified it by saying that he could have relied on 'tried and tested pieces from the past'. Instead he sought to say something new, with the help of others, and he was therefore thankful to those who kept him 'from taking the easy way'. He referred to the chaplain who once prayed 'Lord, make us needful of the minds of others' and remarked that this was 'a good prayer for the all-purpose speaker'. There is another revealing insight into Robert Runcie's methods in this foreword. He writes 'I don't know what I think until I see what I say'. We might contrast a person like Austin Farrer whom I believe would bury his head in his hands for an hour thinking and thinking and then get up and write something. Robert Runcie needed a script before him, actual words which he could probe and push, in order to tease out what he actually thought.

Humphrey Carpenter in his biography seems to pursue the issue of 'ghost writers' almost obsessively, raising it with virtually everyone he interviewed about Runcie.[4] From the points just made a convincing case can be made for saying that despite the extensive use of script writers the final product can quite properly be regarded as belonging to Robert Runcie speaking in his role as Archbishop of Canterbury. It is therefore quite legitimate to take his communications in this period as being his and evaluating them as such.

The mark of Robert Runcie's style can be summed up under a few headings. First, his humour, particularly his self-deprecating humour. He liked nothing better than to begin a sermon or lecture with a story against himself. This was an expression of his essential humility and, as such, it had the effect of immediately breaking down any barriers there might be between the speaker and his audience. People could then relax and be receptive to what might follow.

In Sheffield in 1981 at a conference relating to the 'Ecumenical Decade or the Solidarity of the Church with Women', Runcie began his remarks by saying that he was not sure whether the issue of solidarity with women would have been high on the agenda of the Reformers of the sixteenth century, and particularly pointed to Luther. Not only was there silence but a positive feeling of disenchantment. He learnt afterwards that his remarks and attempts at humour had gone down very badly indeed. It was Mary Tanner who would eventually save the day by offering some further material and by acting as a reconciler. Robert remarked: 'I suppose the lesson to be learned from such an experience is never attempt irony when there are too many Americans from the reformed tradition present!'

Secondly, there is his sense of history. Runcie was a classicist by background and a historian by inclination. He was naturally interested in seeing events and people in their historical context and being interested himself he conveyed something of this interest to other people. He was not naturally either philosophically or theologically minded and he did not like his sermons or lectures to be theologically heavy. There was of course theology in them but this was implicit and understated rather than highlighted. Thirdly, he was most at home on the borderland between the Church and the world, between Christian faith and the wider culture in which it is set. He liked to address secular audiences of any kind. He was socially at ease, without airs or graces, in the company of all manner of people and could relate to their concerns whatever they were. Whether it was a university, the city, a professional association, a civic authority, or a specialist gathering of a particularly esoteric kind, he could speak with ease, without anxiety or affectation. There was a great deal of anxiety, which I will come on to, but it did not arise because of any audience he had to address. Fourthly, he liked to be affirmative, drawing out positive features of the context he was addressing. However secular the audience there was no question of trying to divide the sheep from the goats by any kind of implication or insinuation. Fifthly, this meant that he sought to persuade, rather than exhort or moralize. There was of course a strong Christian message, at once theological and moral, but this was put in such a way as to lead people towards it.

Over his ministry Robert Runcie spoke, preached or lectured on literally thousands of occasions. There is no question of doing justice here to that output. I simply take one or two examples from his time as Archbishop to illustrate these characteristics. On 14 January 1989 he preached a sermon in Birmingham Cathedral as part of a service of thanksgiving to commemorate the centenary of the city's charter. The sermon began:

> The spectacle of the Archbishop of Canterbury preaching in an Anglican cathedral in Birmingham to celebrate the centenary of this city's charter would have confirmed the worst fears of some of its councillors a century ago. They were proud that Birmingham was a city. But there was one serious doubt. It might mean they had to have a Bishop too. A local newspaper reported the anxieties one councillor felt over this dreadful possibility. The Church of England took just 17 years to fulfil his fears and now I stand before you as the consummation of them.

He then dealt quite extensively with some of the history of the city, bringing out some of its distinctive features and remembering some of its famous sons.

> For this city was not born out of a so-called age of faith when cathedral and castle shared a dominance. It has no ancient walls

like London, Chester or York. Its walls are motorways, its main gate Spaghetti Junction. It has no district of Greyfriars nor main thoroughfare of Kirkgate, but there is Gas Street, for it was in Birmingham in 1802 that William Murdoch first made possible the lighting of incandescent mantles.

He affirms the city, the achievements of its leaders and the virtues of its people then he asks why the centenary celebration should begin in a church rather than a public hall. In answer he urged that all human achievements should be rooted in the praise of God and secondly that privileges are always heavy with responsibilities. Then comes a final paragraph:

> Jesus the Jew wept over the city of Jerusalem. His were tears of affection. They were tears that came from knowing how much God had blessed that city and how much he willed it to be a place of his peace. They were tears of sadness as he saw how far that city was from fulfilling its vocation, as it is to this very day. Yet the tears of Jesus were also of longing and resolution, tears forged by his vision of the city where humankind might live in a unity of love. In those tears, he consecrated our local loyalties. Those loyalties we are here to consecrate afresh today – loyalties to this city with its fine traditions, to binding its various communities together into a fellowship marked by enterprise and trust; and care for the less fortunate so that it may be truly said in the word of the Lord to his prophet – 'In this place will I give peace'.

Material for that sermon may have been supplied by Gordon Wakefield, the distinguished Methodist scholar, as Graham James has suggested to me, but as preached it was a sermon characteristic of Runcie at his best. Furthermore, it is difficult to see how a sermon like that could have been preached without the detailed historical knowledge and the feel of Birmingham being supplied by someone who knew them.

I take as another example one of his lectures that he delivered on 19 April 1988 in connection with the Gallipoli memorial service held at Holy Trinity Church, Eltham. He called it 'The God of Battles and the Fight for Faith'.[5] It was a subject on which he was peculiarly well qualified to speak. He was familiar with the terrain and the surrounding seas from his stints as a lecturer on Swan Hellenic cruises. He had also fought through the Second World War, as well as being affected, like all his generation, by memory of the First. The lecture contains many powerful quotations from the First World War poets, notably Wilfred Owen, and, at a more popular level, Studdert Kennedy. He was also fortunate in having access to the seminal study of the Church of England in the First World War by Alan Wilkinson. What is characteristically Runcie about the lecture, however, is his refusal to make easy, platitudinous judgements or to suggest that there are any easy answers to the kind of tragic suffering that the Gallipoli campaign represented. He refused to attribute the Gallipoli campaign to mere adventurism.

> To attribute it to mere adventurism or to engage in easy denunciations of the military planners' disregard for the value of human life would be cynical and rash. I am suspicious of unconsidered, sweeping judgements. Human beings are more often mistaken than callous and my own experience of battle taught me how seriously strategies are considered and how predictive officers are of the men in their charge.

Towards the end when he considers how the First World War destroyed facile notions of providential purpose he points to the poetry of Studdert Kennedy, for whom the cross of Christ, the supreme symbol of God taking our anguish into himself, is the only basis for religious faith. Then he said:

> Personally, I find it difficult to believe in the God of battles, the miracle of Dunkirk, the angel of Mons. For me faith is not believing impossible things. It is trusting that the promises of Christ never fail. It is not hoping the worst will not happen but believing there is no human tragedy which cannot be redeemed – that is, turn to good effect to increase the total output of goodness in the world. In Shakespeare's great play *Henry V* the king says:
> > There is some soul of goodness in things evil,
> > Would men observing distil it out.

War is an evil, messy business but even shared anguish can be a bridge of understanding and ultimate reconciliation. When I attempted to preach on this subject at the service following the Falkland Islands campaign, my subsequent correspondence revealed that it was not the combatants but the commentators who wanted to hear more about the God of battles and less about the fight for faith.

This I think highlights the way Robert Runcie sought to conform to the third of the criteria I posed at the beginning: is it interesting? Is it helpful? Is it true? He avoided overblown rhetoric, claiming too much. His was a faith that had been tried and tempered by experience. He spoke as one with those in their trenches and tanks, not with the more bellicose commentators.

Another set-piece occasion in a setting where Runcie was at his best was the sermon he delivered in the University Church of St Mary the Virgin in Oxford on the occasion of the hundredth anniversary of the death of William Gladstone.[6] It begins, as he liked to, with some personal touch, in this case the memorial library to Gladstone in Hawarden, which he will have visited.

With its decorous gothic architecture set in a small village amidst quiet countryside, it is deceptively tranquil – deceptive, because to stand amidst its books is an intimidating experience, for it is an encounter with the restless, brooding intelligence that was William Ewart Gladstone.

There are characteristic moments of humour, as on the occasion when on the sudden resolution of a particularly knotty crisis in Gladstone's foreign policy the great statesman was able to exclaim, 'God almighty be praised! I can catch the 2.45 to Hawarden'. But the theme of the sermon is deeply serious, namely, Gladstone's profound sense of religious vocation and moral imperative, with Gladstone's manifesto, as it were, being the twelfth chapter of St Paul's letter to the Romans. This was the driving force of Gladstone's life, yet politically he often changed direction, changing from a high Tory in favour of the old order, including establishment, to a Liberal on foreign policy and social affairs. It was Gladstone's conscience which kept him steady amid the changes of political direction, a conscience which led Gladstone to look at issues on their merits. We cannot help feel that there is something of Runcie himself in all this. For by temperament he too was a defender of the old order. He had come into the Christian faith through the spiritual beauty of Anglo-Catholicism and he moved easily with the aristocracy and landed gentry. But he combined these conservative instincts with a rational mind and a liberal outlook that led him, for example, gently towards supporting the ordination of women.

The sermon was extremely well received, not least by the Chancellor of the University, Lord Jenkins, himself a distinguished Gladstone biographer. It was a context which Robert Runcie knew well, one which he knew could be extremely critical and for which therefore he needed to produce something which was academically respectable as well as interesting. All this he was, with his script writer whoever that was, well able to do. But the point is that there was no fooling around. The message was deadly serious. For the service of God is higher than the service of politics, or indeed anything else. A religious vision and profound moral conviction is needed to steer us through the complexities of human existence. Though crafted with great sophistication, the message was essentially simple, and one which no one with ears to hear could miss.

People sometimes accused Robert Runcie of being indecisive – a charge well met by Richard Chartres in his sermon at the memorial service. The positive point behind this impression that he sometimes gave to people was his knowledge that problems we face are often complex and difficult and that, much as we would like it, there are no easy solutions. He knew also both from his time as a soldier in World War Two and his long university experience that the Christian faith is faced by hard questions asked by hard-headed people, that there are subtle and sophisticated minds that need to be opened to gospel truths. It is not surprising therefore that in one of his very first interviews as Archbishop of Canterbury he stressed the fact that he was not going to provide simple answers, that there were several sides to each question and that it was important for Christian leaders to grapple with reality as it is in all its complexity rather than pretend that all difficulties will dissolve before some simplistic solution. Together with this awareness, which was fundamental to Robert Runcie's outlook and which helped shape everything he said, was a strong desire, to put it very simply, to do his best: to do his best for God, for the Church for which he was an official spokesperson, and for himself. Those who fail to see that Robert Runcie was powerfully driven by a deep religious faith fail to understand the man. He wanted to serve the God in whom he believed as well as he could. Furthermore, he knew that the Church was often pilloried and caricatured. He wanted what he said to have credibility for the sake of the Church. It was a question of honour. The question of honour was important too in his desire to do the best for himself. His war service will have given him a strong sense of what was required of an officer, encapsulated in phrases like not letting the regiment down, or not letting the men down. This sense of honour combined with anxieties in himself about not letting himself down, that is, not appearing to others as a fool. This is not the place to dwell on those anxieties but the result was that he worked hard to produce his best on every occasion that he could. His best for God, his best for the regiment, that is, the Church, his best for himself because he did not want to let himself down either.

The range of public speaking engagements lined up before him weighed heavily on Runcie's mind. The mention of one a few days or a week or so ahead would bring forth the retort, 'There are many hurdles to jump before that one'. This desire to produce something worthy for public engagements, together with his willingness to give himself unstintingly to the people he was with at any time, meant that he worked extremely hard indeed. When I was with him in 1987 in Singapore for the seventh meeting of the Anglican Consultative Council I almost had forcibly to march him away from the pressing throng to spend 20 minutes swimming in a local hotel pool. Without that, he would simply have allowed himself to have yet more photos taken of himself with delegates or listen to yet another problem from somewhere in the Anglican Communion.

It mattered very much to Runcie that his public lectures,

sermons and other forms of communication were good and, whatever he used in the way of help, he worked hard to make them as good as possible. Paradoxically, one of the reasons why he liked to have a very carefully wrought script, in which he could feel confident, was that this enabled him to relax a little and attend to the people he was with on that occasion. For, again, paradoxically, he once said, 'It's better to arrive on good form than well prepared'. But he knew that if he was well prepared he was much more likely to arrive on good form.

Those who knew Robert Runcie believe that he was a very great human being. This was, quite simply, because he was a person-orientated person. He never wrote the book at Cambridge that people thought he ought to be writing and about which he sometimes felt embarrassed because he was giving himself to people. He had the extraordinary ability to home into where people were within a few seconds. To watch him work a large hall, as for instance I did when I was Dean of King's College, London, and the Archbishop paid an official visit, was to be filled with admiration. He could move from a cleaner, whom he would immediately discover had lived next door to his parents in Liverpool, to a professor of ancient history and feel equally at ease with both and find he had things in common with both. This extraordinary, intuitive capacity, developed by his Christian faith, to enter sympathetically into the feelings and perceptions of other people comes out not only in his relationships with others but in his communications. As already mentioned, it meant that he could do superb vignettes of people which made those who heard them instantly recognize the person concerned, affectionately laugh at their foibles and respect their contribution. This quality meant that some of Robert Runcie's best sermons and lectures were those about other people. A good example of this is the sermon he preached at the Memorial Eucharist for Sister Jane of the Divine Compassion SLG, who was formerly the Revd Mother of the Sisters of the Love of God. This sermon focuses on Jane, her humour for example. 'She did feel that people without a sense of humour lacked a sense of proportion and should never be put in charge of anything – especially a country or a community.' Again, 'Jane was suspicious of the low blink rate, the shining eyes or the

spring in the stride of a zealot'. While outraged by the injustices
of the world she warned an angry campaigner,

> It is important not to get bogged down in one's impotence to
> alleviate human misery so that you forget the good things in
> life that matter so much; lots of people are happy and God
> is glad for them and with them.

Robert admires and celebrates her capacity to say very simple
things which, because they came from her, were entirely credible
and profound. She loved the phrase 'The undefeated heart of
weakness'. In such a sermon the preacher himself becomes trans-
parent. His ego does not intrude. When C. S. Lewis introduced
an American edition of sermons by Austin Farrer he began by
wondering why there were so few books like it. He ended:

> Perhaps, after all, it is not so difficult to explain why books
> like this are rare. For one thing, the work involved is very
> severe; not the work of this or that essay but the life-long
> work without which they could not even have begun. For
> another, they demand something like a total conquest of those
> egoisms which – however we try to mince the matter – play
> so large a part in most impulses to authorship. To talk to
> us about Dr Farrer makes himself almost nothing, almost a
> nobody. To be sure, in the event, his personality stands out
> from the pages as clearly as that of any author; but this is
> one of heaven's jokes – nothing makes a man so noticeable
> as vanishing.[7]

This capacity to laugh with whose who laugh and cry with those
who cry means that however important Robert Runcie's public
forms of communications were his most distinctive and in the
end most influential expression of Christian truth was suggested
by the quotations from Malcolm Lesiter and Bob Hardy.
Andrew Brown wrote in his splendid obituary in *The Independent* (see pp. 127–36):

> One example that I discovered by chance: he wrote letters
> every day for months to a mutual friend hospitalized with

cancer. This was at a time when he was involved in the running of the General Synod, the Canterbury Diocese, the Primates' meeting and planning the run-up to the Lambeth Conference, as well as several other full-time jobs.

Someone, at sometime, has a wonderful opportunity before them: to produce a collection of Bob Runcie's letters. Here, above all, he will be seen truly to have come into his own as a Christian communicator.

On 24 October 1981 Robert Runcie came to Grays Court in Oxfordshire to dedicate the Archbishop's maze for an old friend. He composed prayers specially for the occasion, one of which reads:

Lord God, we thank thee for all that thou hast fashioned here to remind us of the beauty of your creation, the mystery of time and eternity and the signs you have given us of your love for all mankind.

Help us to find our way through the path of life with simplicity, courage, and truth. Lift from our hearts all anxiety and fear. So ever more lead us in thy way and keep us in thy peace through Jesus Christ our Lord.

8. Cruise Control: Runcie at Sea with Swan

ANTHONY BRYER

I first met Robert Runcie in summer 1968 on his own ground, coming off the cricket pitch at Cuddesdon to scattered applause from the deckchairs. The Principal had made a studied and stylish innings and was happy in the sun. Over the next 30 years he was to make the Mediterranean his own ground, when he could, to the same discreet and discretely shared delight. This is just a happy story, but Robert himself found it important, which may say something.

We met because we had both been invited as Guest Lecturers on our first Swan Hellenic Cruise and were apprehensive. It was reassuring that 'Guest' meant that we were expected to bring wives, described as 'librarians', in a supporting role. Female lecturers were introduced quite early and painlessly in our time – bringing husbands with their watercolours as 'librarians'. It was Lindy Runcie who was to pioneer the next logical step, as ship's professional pianist who brought her spouse along too. But in 1968 there was a one-man band who thumped out 'Never on a Sunday'. Robert could not resist spotting other analogies with the Church of England, which developed over the years, mostly deceptive. I start with simple terminology. Despite common usage, 'HC' henceforth indicates Hellenic Cruise, and *pax* = Passengers.

I forget which political party or social class the Church of England was supposed to represent at prayer, but at sea in the sun Sir Henry Lunn, a former Methodist missionary, did not. He knew precisely who his *pax* were when he launched the first HC to Troy and the isles of Greece on 16 April 1908. By 1910 Lunn's Hellenic Travellers' Club listed over 2500 subscribers by civil rank. They were a captive audience for guest lecturers who included the sounder members of the bench of bishops, the better sort of Greats don, some capital clerical public school headmasters – and not many Methodist missionaries. Yet there was an assumed mission statement: that *pax* were on ordered pilgrimage to a conception of fifth-century Athens, were allowed to botanize on Hymettos on the way, and dressed for dinner amid the amusing discomforts of the boat. But in 1911 Lunn was astute enough to appoint W. F. Swan as his assistant.

From 1954 W. F. Swan and his son, R. Ken Swan, revived Hellenic Cruises for the Club. By then other things may have changed, but the objectives of Troy, the isles of Greece and a conception of fifth-century Athens were consistent, for they could still be reached by sea in sterling. Even more constant seems to have been an unwritten understanding that when at sea the ship was C of E. One guest lecturer was designated padre, whose duties were laid down by Canon Guy Pentreath, a capital public school headmaster and secretary of the Hellenic Travellers' Club. The padre officiated at an altar draped with the Union flag, to distinguish it from other tables in the bar, was licensed to read Acts 19.23–41 in the theatre at Ephesus and (until 1974) to cast a wreath on the Dardanelles with the (then Turkish) captain as the ship passed Gallipoli.

An analogy with the Church of England is the interesting question of preferment. Our appointments were signed by Sir Mortimer Wheeler, Ken Swan's academic partner, on the writing paper of his other job as Secretary of the British Academy in Burlington House. In 1968 Robert guessed that a Chadwick was behind his preferment – they say that he was also offered the deanery of Guildford that year. I knew precisely why I had been recruited. In 1967 I had managed to get permission to work on and in the upper chamber of the Chrysokephalos, the coronation cathedral of the emperors of Trebizond. Since 1461 it has been the principal mosque of Trabzon, a quiet place – until Swan Hellenic first burst upon the Black Sea. On 16 August 1967 the imam appeared in the upper chamber, agitated. He said there was a commotion outside, waves of shameless female infidels. I went down to find Wheeler holding forth to a crowd of tourists with yellow badges on their walking sticks. He was talking nonsense. I sided with the imam, who had the advantage of the minaret microphone to summon support. On his side Wheeler had a Chadwick (Henry, he said). But we negotiated a peek into the mosque for the tourists in chaperoned groups before they sailed off. A consequence was that I found, poste restante, Trabzon, a summons from Wheeler to accompany the next Euxine cruise, HC 77 (1968), with the Principal of Cuddesdon as padre.

HC 77 gyrated clockwise round the Black Sea from 20 August to 3 September 1968. There is something special about everyone's first HC, but this was truly wonderful and 30 years later we found our synoptic memories of it still shining. Although HC 77 wisely skipped Trabzon, it was an astonishingly imaginative itinerary which, since the collapse of the Soviet Union, can probably not be repeated. But Hellenic Cruises have traditionally sailed through political trouble, beginning in 1908 when the Young Turks staged a revolution in Istanbul and the Cretans rose, while *pax* at sea blithely debated the relative merits of Athenian and British Imperialism. In 1968 Robert recalled that things began quietly enough, though he claimed he was more concerned about making a good impression on Miss Doreen Goodrick, the formidable cruise director with a heart of gold. In Istanbul I remember Mrs K. I. Essayan kindly offering a Turkish brandy (called *Kanyak*) to any lecturer willing to discuss Armenia, and on 21 August Robert recalled hearing something on BBC World News about a Soviet invasion of Czechoslovakia, but both were small distant countries not on the itinerary. However, by 23 August Russian tanks were in Prague. Dubček had made a pact with Romania, but Bulgaria supported Brezhnev and we were in Bulgaria. Here in a resort called 'Sunny Beach' the Czech wife of Maurice Broomfield, photographer lecturer, was approached by bewildered Czech holidaymakers who had been rounded up and wanted to know what was going on. It all became very real: time for Swan himself to fly in to sort things out. Robert noted that there was plenty of advice available on board, for *pax* happened to include Lord Carrington and the ambassadors of Spain and Peru. HC 77 held unwavering course for Russia. In Odessa some *pax* climbed the steps, watching out for hurtling prams, and others flew, as programmed, on an 'optional' excursion to Moscow, where Dubček (who had no option) also arrived on 24 August. Meanwhile in the Crimea Maurice Broomfield photographed us impersonating Churchill, Stalin and Roosevelt on the bench at Yalta, which was reassuringly twinned with Margate. But Swan's Greek guides Hypatia and Maria were not allowed ashore, so we were taken past gleaming tsarist palaces by an Intourist guide who explained that they were now all workers' sanatoria. Robert recalled Maureen, Marchioness of Dufferin and Ava, enquiring with anxious concern: 'And what is ailing your poor workers?' Today the palatial sanatoria are the country seats of the 'new' mafia.

On 29 August HC 77 berthed at Sochi, whence another 'optional' excursion flew (just) over the snowy Caucasus. In a packed day in Tbilisi we saw the medieval enamels which Stalin had repatriated to Georgia but are now thought to have been made by Fabergé in St Petersburg all along, and in Mtskheta met some centenarians who looked authentic too. Dinner was in the Mtatsminda Restaurant on Mount David, high above the city. Here the food did not quite match the view, which was spectacular. Ever caring of his *pax*, Swan complained. Its management explained that the Mtatsminda was only licensed as a Grade II restaurant and obligingly served the same meal (and wines) all over again. Having overcome much greater obstacles, Ken Swan was caught off guard by this classic Caucasian gambit. But *pax* redoubled their toasts in preparation for the next adventure, which was the midnight sleeper to Colchis. At that hour Tbilisi Railway Station was unforgettable.

It was a packed night. There was so much to do, pulling out bunks, fiddling with samovars, glimpsing Stalin's birthplace in Gori and speculating when we would be ambushed. We were not ambushed until dawn. The train was held up by the sea near Batum. Swan's sleeping cars were surrounded by Young Pioneers in red scarves – bearing bouquets for the ladies and brandy for the parson. Today they say that the 'new' mafia are selling the very rail track, second hand.

From Batum to Athens should have been plain sailing all the way down the Bosphorus, but Robert always maintained that his time of trial came on the last day of HC 77. In Swan Annals, or *The Runciad*, the story has become canonical, but I was there and am sticking to mine. It had been a packed morning in Athens and Robert returned to the ship in Piraeus to snatch a siesta before his afternoon assignment, an excursion to Sounion – unaware that the bus left from Athens. The quiet ship was woken by a broadcast announcement: 'Where's that bloody padre!?' Miss Goodrick had (she said inadvertently) left the microphone switched on. I witnessed Robert erupt from the cabin opposite. There was an epic taxi chase, and applause on time in Sounion. In today's traffic he would not have had a hope.

When asked about his other life as a cruise lecturer, Robert would relate the Sounion story and go into a self-deprecatory routine about being an amateur among academics (*Ho! Ho!*) and not being able to distinguish a caryatid from a Berkshire pig (*Ho! Ho! Ho!*). Robert Runcie was, of course, a peerless cruise lecturer, as anyone who heard him ashore might guess, and the freedom of the sea released his waggishness. He was in palpable touch with his audience and could change gear from the confiding to the magisterial mode in mid-sentence. At sea, *pax* are a conspiracy of Insiders, who nevertheless seek real-life Authority. Robert enjoyed the ambiguous status of guest lecturer, wondering whether to put out his shoes or polish the others. I think he also enjoyed (certainly made much of) the humility of the extra-mural teacher who must assume that there is always someone who knows more about any one topic than he. In Robert's *progymnasmata* humility was more than a rhetorical device. In 1967 Wheeler had dismissed his troops in Trabzon as '*pax* catching up on a classical education they never had'. But Robert was as respectful of his troops as was the Iron Duke. He worked harder, professionally, for them than he cared to admit. At sea he had necessarily few clerical witnesses and Lindy was his only minder. Was that the attraction? Robert was indeed quoted as saying, in an unguarded hour, that 'I was ashamed that I got more delight from lecturing on a Swan Hellenic cruise than I did from going to some religious rally.' I venture that the real attraction was simpler and more positive. Robert was a natural didact. Give a don a talk on a good site in good company and he is away. In the theatre at Ephesus there is all too much to see and say, but the simple mound at Marathon requires more than a *Thought for the Day*. It is more tricky than it sounds. In those years it was a quite strenuous job too. Until 1974 the cruise ship could not accommodate all *pax* together, so lecturers had to repeat their talks. Robert found his *pax* following him from bar to dining room for a second sitting, which, in the spirit of the Mtatsminda restaurant he obliged, but with a fresh meal. In 1970 Robert pioneered what remains the ultimate labour of Swan: a three-hour commentary on the monasteries of Mount Athos as the ship 'close cruises' the peninsula. I confess that I had doubts about such ecclesiastical voyeurism. Would an anchorite, who had left the world, welcome shameless women with binoculars – some doubtless infidel or (worse) schismatic, sailing (worst of all) under a Turkish flag? Further, Robert had not himself then set foot on the Holy Mountain. You are all at sea if you miss the first of 20 monasteries in sequence, for there is one left to account for at the end. But in truth Athonite monks are just as curious of the other world and seize any chance of evangelizing – one (my former student in England) would rush to the bells as we passed. And in truth by 1970 Robert was deeply involved in consultations with the Orthodox Church. He spoke not just with sympathy but authority. Sometimes to their surprise, people found that 'close-cruising' Athos with Robert Runcie was a profound experience which none can forget.

After the first Athonite marathon in 1970, Robert could not forget that Miss Goodrick sent him champagne for dinner that night. He said it made up for the Sounion incident of 1968, which he claimed was why he had not been asked to lecture in 1969, when all that came was an invitation to St Albans. It was, of course, a nonsense – how sensitive could Robert be? In truth he and Doreen Goodrick became firm friends, with the mutual respect of professionals who know their respective jobs. Ken Swan and Robert Runcie shared war-time experience too. Both knew what a military movement order was (the clue to Swan logistics), but I think that what Runcie most appreciated in Swan was his relish for crisis – when to risk an imaginative decision and sail calmly on to Russia.

The Bishop of St Albans continued cruise lecturing during his decade there. They were, perhaps, his halcyon days in both offices – to the refreshment of both. I am told that the Berkshire pigs were happy too. But on 19 July 1979 another invitation arrived at St Albans – from Mrs Thatcher. The Runcies went to Italy to consider it. *Pax*, of course, knew nothing of this until 23 August when HC 171 disembarked at Venice, to find them incognito at Marco Polo airport, hitch-hiking home care of Swan. I noticed Robert deep in conversation with a Chadwick (Henry), but in awful silence Lindy took me aside to point at the name she had noticed on the waiting plane. It was *The Canterbury Belle.*

The Archbishop of Canterbury did not lecture on cruises during his decade there, though I did notice his diocesans and chaplains among ship's padres, for Robert Runcie could not but help keep in touch – sometimes quite literally. Processing down Toronto cathedral in full canonicals he felt a tug from *pax* in a pew: 'Remember me? Cruise 123.' Given a chance, communications remained open. In August 1980 the Pope may have been unaware that the Archbishop's invitation to visit Canterbury came in part through spasmodic marine radio from a Swan's guest *pax* somewhere in the Mediterranean. I fancy that Lord Carrington and a Chadwick (Henry again) came into that story too.

In 1985 the invitation to Swan's Last Cruise came from the Archbishop of Canterbury and the President of the British Academy, who was a Chadwick (Owen this time). Tickets and yellow badges were issued for 1 October. Ken and Marion Swan were embarked at the Tower of London. There was a running commentary down the Thames and deck talks galore. What do you expect of 100 lecturers on a boat? Mr Terry Waite held up the traffic for us at Lambeth Pier and handed canapés at the party in the Palace, round which there was an unusually guided tour, much oratory and redoubled toasts. Of course Ken Swan's retirement in 1985 and Robert Runcie's in 1991 were both somewhat nominal and they were soon at it again, still working wonders. How else in 1994 could Robert have taken a funeral in Nottingham while sailing from Malta to Carthage?

HC 496 sailed from 21 October to 4 November 1997 and was, I think, Robert's penultimate cruise. He knew he was ill, but visited the Seven Sleepers at Ephesus and climbed the Krak des Chevaliers. The Swans were there and the itinerary was as imaginative as ever: St Symeon the Stylite, Apamea and Aleppo, Damascus and Palmyra (where it rained). Hizbollah claimed toll on the road to Baalbek and Beirut looked like a ravaged yet animated cheese. Robert sent a picture postcard of the rue Weygand before the war. It began 'Dear Terry...' (well, you are allowed to read other people's postcards).

HC 496 was, however, chiefly memorable for two lectures which Robert gave. The first was entitled, innocently enough: 'The Quest for Father Christmas'. This was serious. In fact Robert had been doing research on the confused iconography and archaeology, miracles and cults, of St Nicholas of Myra and St Nicholas of Sion for some time. He had the excavation reports at his fingertips – where they may have remained, for they are in Japanese. But two years before, he had slipped his minders for three hours in Philadelphia to visit a Byzantinist who was working on the same problems. He wrote to me: 'What a gentle and wondrous scholar – I felt lifted out of worldly cares as well as provided with many fresh insights (and some impressive slides).' She wrote to me: 'What a wonderful man. I have never met anyone like him. I wanted to ask him so much but he had all the questions and there was no time.'

Robert's final lecture on HC 496 was entitled 'Beirut and the Hostage Story'. This was not just serious, but unprecedented. Canon Pentreath's 'Notes for Swan Lecturers' once included instruction about wearing ties and avoiding talking about anything interesting, like theology, sex or politics – although he used to suggest a title of an uncontroversial lecture to be delivered at Dubrovnik: 'Yugoslavia: Five Republics, Four Languages, Three Religions, Two Alphabets, One People'.

If Robert put much research into his St Nicholas lecture, the emotional energy and apprehension that went into 'Beirut and the Hostage Story' was almost painfully evident. He had been planning it with deliberation for some time. One felt that he wanted to unburden himself and that he felt that this was the right place to do it. In the enclosed world of a cruise, lectures are off-the-record and no hostage is taken. I can only report that this lecture was controlled, scholarly (we learned much more about Hizbollah) and that there was no joke – or mention by name of Mr Waite.

Dr Runcie's enthronement at St Alban's in 1970 had been attended by a scattering of ex-*pax*. Lord Runcie's funeral at

St Albans on 22 July 2000 brought them out in droves, headed by the Swans. There were almost as many guest lecturers as bishops – well some were both. Robert had made a studied, stylish – and inspiring – innings. He had been happy in the sun and made *pax* of us all.

PART THREE

An Archbishop's Life

9. Remembering a Good Man[1]

ANDREW BROWN

Robert Runcie was a good man doing an impossible job in a bad time. Very probably, he was the last Archbishop of Canterbury who had the stature and the experience to be an integral part of the Establishment in its secular sense. But his public position was not nearly as remarkable as his personal qualities. It's not the Establishment that matters: almost everyone who knew him will feel that they would swap half the British constitution to have him back.

He was born in 1921 in Birkenhead, the son of Robert Dalziel Runcie, an electrical engineer who, when Robert was 17, went blind and had to take early retirement from his position at Tate & Lyle. This meant that the family home – a semi-detached house without grandeur – had to be sold. Such a background was much lower down the social scale than that of most of his predecessors as Archbishop. It may have contributed to the impression he could give many people of being absent. He played innumerable roles very well indeed, but there could be a quality of awkwardness and not belonging about him, which television ruthlessly ferreted out.

By the time catastrophe overwhelmed his parents, Runcie was already on his way to Oxford University, as a scholarship boy. The word 'gentleman' is so bound up with snobbery, and Runcie was so much a gentleman, in his bearing as well as his acts, that it is difficult for anyone who knew him as Archbishop to imagine him as the son of an electrical engineer and a ship's hairdresser, in Birkenhead.

Cleverness was his first route out. But he was also a gifted cricketer, and, according to one biographer, a brilliant mimic. His home was not a religious one: in the manner of the English middle classes, occasional church attendance was used as a vaccination against belief. In Runcie, however, the effects of this were overcome by his headmaster, a serious and devout man who gave him works of biblical criticism to read.

Other people's faith is as much a mystery as their marriages, yet it seems that the two most important facts about Runcie's religious formation were that it was never dramatic or theatrical – it started as an intellectual conviction informed by historical criticism – and that it had, very early, to contend with the hideous fate suffered by his father. These things taken together seem to have quite inoculated him against triumphalism. When he was Archbishop, he was constantly to be assailed with demands to 'give a clear lead'. These calls were wholly futile: even if the Church of England were a body capable of being led in any direction, as Runcie knew better than anyone it was not; had the English in the 1980s been a nation given to fellowship, as even Margaret Thatcher found they were not, he could not have risen to declamatory dogmatism.

War service seems to have reinforced this thoughtful, profoundly unrhetorical side of him. After one undergraduate year at Brasenose College he was commissioned into the Scots Guards, where he did extremely well. He was brave, competent, and well liked. He fought his way across northern France and Germany in the wake of D-Day. In March 1945 he won the Military Cross for two successive feats of bravery: first, rescuing one of his men from a crippled tank under heavy enemy fire; and the next day taking his own tank into an exceptionally exposed position in order to knock out three anti-tank guns.

In May 1945 he was among the first British troops to enter Belsen. Much later, in a speech, he remarked that the Second World War had been worth fighting in order to put an end to Belsen but, he added with a historian's scruple characteristically destructive of rhetoric, that was not why it had been fought.

None of his army friends guessed that he had settled his heart on ordination after the war. But after a First in Greats at Oxford, he went to Westcott House, in Cambridge. Oxford philosophy was then in the throes of logical positivism, a philosophy which marked deeply many of the more thoughtful members of the Church of England of that generation. They might in the end conclude that metaphysical discussion was possible and even necessary, whatever A. J. Ayer might believe, but they would never feel happy with large metaphysical constructions such as the fortifications which surround the opinions of Pope John Paul II and their gimcrack equivalents in the Church of England. This would lead to difficulty later, over the ordination of women.

He was ordained deacon on Christmas Day 1950, priest a year later, and served two years as a curate on Tyneside before returning to Westcott as chaplain. He was then promoted to Vice-Principal; in 1956, Owen Chadwick picked Runcie to be his successor as Dean of Trinity Hall, and John Habgood succeeded to Runcie's place at Westcott. It makes a pleasant picture of three men who were to become among the most influential in the Church of England forming up like railroad cars along the fast track.

At Trinity Hall, Runcie married Lindy Turner, the daughter of a law don, who met him as his secretary there. Some of his staff at Lambeth Palace found her a trial, but it is hardly the principal job of a wife to appear agreeable to her husband's connections. She could give the impression that she thought almost everyone who talked to him was wasting his time; she may have been right. Loyal herself, she resented fiercely the disloyalty endemic to journalism and politics. The couple had two children.

From Trinity Hall, he continued, onwards and upwards, to become Principal of Cuddesdon, the Oxford equivalent of Westcott House. He spent 10 years there, developing the habits of work that were to rescue him as Archbishop, but in an institution curiously untouched by the ferment of the Sixties. Runcie did a little to mitigate its organized misogyny. When he arrived, married ordinands were expected to keep their families at least two miles from the place, to spend all day, from 7 a.m. until 9.30 p.m., in the seminary, and to keep Saturday lunch as their only meal of the week with the family. There had been some small relaxation in this discipline when he left.

In 1970 he was consecrated Bishop of St Albans. It rapidly became apparent that he was the most able as well as one of the most liked men within the Church of England. It is said that he turned down the see of York in 1975; in 1980 he was distressed to be offered the see of Canterbury. He felt he must accept: he was the first man to be chosen by the new Crown

Appointments Commission, and to that extent represented the choice of the Church and not the Prime Minister.

The drawbacks of the post as they might have presented themselves to him are many: the first is the disorganization of the Church of England. An Archbishop of Canterbury has little more power than the King of Poland. In the phrase used by John V. Taylor, the saintly Bishop of Winchester, after he had chaired a doctrine commission, to lead such a body is like taking a large collection of dogs for a walk in the country without enough leads. In the case of the Anglican Communion, of which the Archbishop is a sort of primate, the analogy may be extended: the pack of good-natured, energetic, English dogs is augmented by an elephant or two, some very touchy rodents and perhaps a hippogriff.

It is a further drawback to the job that this powerlessness is not publicly recognized. The Archbishop will be held responsible for any sheep worried, exactly as if he had personally urged the unleashed animals on. The period of Runcie's primacy was to be one of profound divergences and strains within the Church. The issues involved were common to the whole of Christianity, but in the Church of England, which had acquired the institutions to do everything with decisions except take them, the effects seemed particularly severe.

The battles between liberal and a resurgent conservative theology, which concentrated in this period on belief in miracle stories, revealed that the Church of England contained men who did not even pretend to believe any of them and men who would pretend to believe in everything they were ever told. It is hard to tell which faction damaged more the kind of reasonable, humane belief whose possibilities Runcie always upheld.

Only one of the problems facing an archbishop could not have appeared to him, then, in its full horror: the fact that Margaret Thatcher was going to be his Prime Minister. Her choice of an appointments secretary seemed to Runcie evidence of an evangelical plot to do down good Catholic liberals everywhere.

All these difficulties were to come together in the great crisis of his primacy, the *Crockford's* affair. But, while that dramatized the issues involved, it did little or nothing to resolve them.

Any attempt to solve them, or to live with them, is complicated by the logical incoherence of the Church of England. The problem is not that there are no good answers to the questions 'What is the Church of England for?' and 'Why is it here?' There are a number of very good answers, all accepted by different bits of the Church, and all profoundly incompatible with each other.

It now seems that these are not problems at all, but conflicts. The difference is that problems have solutions; while conflicts only have outcomes. It may have been the profoundest weakness of Runcie's primacy and of the church he led to see problems where there were in fact profound and insoluble conflicts; but in the Eighties he was for a while a kind of unofficial leader of the Opposition to a government which saw all problems as conflicts.

Runcie, for all his adult life, had believed that the Church of England is a part of Catholic Christendom. The first spectacular act of his primacy was a dramatic demonstration of this. Meeting Pope John Paul in Accra, when both men were on African visits, he invited him to visit Canterbury Cathedral. 'We have a martyr there who would interest you', he said, a wonderful example of the judgement behind his charm: what Pole under Communism could resist the shrine of Thomas à Becket, who died to defend the papacy against a secular power?

The Pope's visit to Canterbury in 1982 was postponed by the Falklands War. But when it came, it was as close as we may ever get to a Roman Catholic recognition of the Church of England as a real, Catholic church. It may have marked a profound change in English self-understanding: English patriotism has long been entwined with anti-Catholicism. The wilder rantings of Ian Paisley would have made perfect sense to almost everyone in Britain 100 years ago. Runcie's gracious, generous and intelligent handling of these matters was hugely important in showing that attitudes had changed, as well as in changing them.

In the meantime, the war that had postponed the Pope's visit had supplied Runcie with his first political crisis. His sermon at the service of thanksgiving in St Paul's was praised by Willie Whitelaw (who had served with him in the Scots Guards), but grossly offended against the braying triumphalist spirit that then possessed the Conservative Party. The ostensible offence was that the Archbishop had remembered the Argentinian dead as well as our own. But there was a deeper objection, too: the reflective, unrhetorical style of his sermon could never have satisfied people who felt the world needed remythologizing, whatever he actually said. His sermon is the work of a man who, after he won his Military Cross, walked over the battlefield to look at the bodies of the men he had killed.

It is not the way of politicians to contemplate the bodies of their victims. The reaction to the Archbishop's next journey into political life reflected this: the report of a commission he had set up to study the inner cities and the Church's role in them was travestied as 'Marxist theology' by a cabinet minister.

Runcie, a man to whom the courtesies of the Establishment were second nature, now found himself pilloried as a wimpish outsider. In 1984 the consecration of David Jenkins as Bishop of Durham gave pleasure and profit to the opponents of liberalism everywhere. Jenkins's opinions were widely believed to be intolerable when they were mostly incoherent. It might be observed that it is the duty of any Archbishop to defend the incoherence of the Church of England; but the impression was left that the Church of England under Runcie was a place where anyone could believe anything. *Private Eye* put the Archbishop on its cover, saying, 'With men like us, who needs women priests?' At the same time his ceaseless travels and his great energies were making him more personal friends than any other Archbishop may have had. One example, that I discovered by chance: he wrote letters every day for months to a mutual friend hospitalized with cancer. This was at a time when he was involved in the running of the General Synod, the Canterbury Diocese, the Primates' meeting and planning the run-up to the Lambeth Conference, as well as several other full-time jobs. There came to be an almost unbridgeable divide between the Archbishop as he was portrayed and the man in the flesh, possessed of tremendous natural authority.

He had put the workings of Lambeth Palace on to an almost professional basis. He used speechwriters from all over the academic community, but he had a knack of mastering their briefs completely. Among his not entirely successful innovations was the hiring of Terry Waite as his Secretary for Anglican Communion Affairs. In due course, after Waite became involved far more deeply than he should have done with the American adventures in the Middle East, John Lyttle, an exceptionally tough-minded and experienced man from the SDP, was hired to bring him back under control and manage the palace's relations with government.

In the event, Waite was kidnapped two days after Lyttle started his new job. Had Runcie known all the details that were to emerge later, he would almost certainly have tried harder to stop Waite from leaving on his final trip. He reproached himself bitterly afterwards, and he was greatly persecuted by his enemies in the press, for whom the apparently uncomplicated and certainly unintellectual figure of Waite made a much finer model of Christian leadership. This idea was attractive to Waite himself in some moods.

By the winter of 1987, when Waite was kidnapped, Runcie had made friends all over the world, and acquired enemies in all parties of Church and State. The hostility to him among the jackals of the Conservative Party has already been noted. The *Daily Star* published that summer a series of articles about Lindy Runcie, based on the testimony of disgruntled ex-employees, that earned her quite a lot of money when her libel action was settled out of court.

Thoughtful Conservatives, too, found Runcie unsympathetic to all grand designs for the remoralization of society, and within the parties of the Church there were few who could not consider themselves slighted. The emergence of the General Synod as a body whose debates could, on occasion, command the attention of the whole nation, suggested opportunities to a number of politicians, both clergy and lay, who felt that they, too, deserved this attention.

The first crisis came over homosexuals. In the spring of 1987, the Revd Tony Higton, an Essex vicar who had been prominent in the agitation against the Bishop of Durham, put down a private motion calling for a return to 'biblical standards of morality' among Church leaders. This caught the evangelical imagination and, despite vigorous efforts to block it from behind the scenes, the motion was given a full debate in November that year. The Church was profoundly confused as well as divided over the issue. In the event, the Synod was able to pretend to unite around a motion which condemned 'homosexual genital acts' but not the condition of homosexuality. This laid the ground for another decade of trench warfare, without satisfying anyone: 'Pulpit Poofs Must Stay', proclaimed the next day's headline in the *Sun*.

The anonymous preface to *Crockford's Clerical Directory* was a piece of well-informed cattiness that had for 10 years been written by the liberal historian David Edwards, the Provost of Southwark. When he dropped the job, Derek Pattinson, who had run the Church of England's General Synod almost since its inception, offered it to a Conservative historian in holy orders, Gary Bennett, of New College, Oxford. Bennett had been a pupil and friend of Runcie's at Westcott House, and was later one of his speechwriters. In later life, disappointed of both clerical and academic advancement, he threw himself into synodical politics. He wrote with elegance, penetration and ferocious malice.

The centrepiece of the preface that he finally submitted for the 1987 edition of *Crockford's* was a portrait of Runcie which started by quoting Frank Field's epigram 'The Archbishop is usually to be found nailing his colours to the fence', and went on in tones to make that opening seem eirenic. Runcie was accused of lacking all principle, and of systematically corrupting the Church by appointing only cronies to the bench of bishops.

The author's identity was spotted by anyone who knew him as soon as they read the preface. He started lying to the press about it on the day of publication, when the savage personal attack on Runcie in an official church publication was front-page news in almost all the papers. Bennett killed himself four days later, when his exposure seemed certain. Of all the actors in the affair, Runcie alone emerged with his reputation enhanced. He did so by saying nothing at all in public.

The specific accusations of jobbery were disproved, by painstaking research; of the four most ardent 'traditionalist' supporters of Gary Bennett's thesis, one was blown up by the *News of the World*; another lost his synod seat after circulating copies of the *News of the World* article in question to every other member of the Synod; a third became a Roman Catholic journalist and a fourth an Archdeacon of York.

The next year brought the Lambeth Conference. Every 10 years, hundreds of Anglican bishops from all over the world gather at Canterbury. The Anglican Communion is one of the largest Christian bodies in the world, and the Archbishop of Canterbury is its head. But neither he, nor any other body in the Communion, has anything approaching disciplinary powers. The churches involved do what seems best to them, over the ordination of women and much else.

No one was certain what, under these circumstances, 'communion' meant. Now, of course, it is obvious that it means nothing at all; but in 1988 everyone who saw Runcie at that conference, working constantly, listening, teaching, exhorting and laughing, thought that communion was what he established with his presence. He spread joy and respect among everyone he talked to. It was at once a demonstration and a justification of all his searching for unity. He did not, I think, fool himself. 'The secret of being Archbishop of Canterbury', he said, years later, 'is never to believe your own propaganda', and he came to believe that the Anglican Communion was not an organization to be taken seriously.

In the seventies and eighties there was no power on earth or elsewhere that could have brought about substantial agreement on the issue of women priests within any of the Western churches. It was Runcie's misfortune to have been Archbishop at the moment when the Church of England could no longer dodge the question. He moved slowly towards a whole-hearted acceptance of women as priests and bishops; he had never, I think, doubted that they would come in the end, but towards the end of his primacy he believed that delay was wrong. Opinion in the General Synod did not follow him. In 1989, when legislation with a real chance of success was at last introduced to the General Synod, he voted against it because it was, he said, 'legislation for schism'. But schism, it turned out, was what the opposition wanted and has largely got.

On his last visit to Rome, he left behind him a storm of Protestant outrage, because he had said that the whole Church needed a primacy that could only be exercised by a Bishop of

Rome, though the papacy of Runcie's vision was far too Anglican, conciliar and collegiate for any real pope to accept, as his
host made abundantly clear.

In retirement he remained as charming as ever, and rather
more indiscreet. He got into trouble by allowing the writer
Humphrey Carpenter to tape a series of conversations in which
his personality and opinions came across with un-archiepiscopal
force and candour. Runcie had thought that nothing would be
published until he was dead; but Carpenter had a contract to
fulfil and in his *Robert Runcie: A Reluctant Archbishop* (1996)
produced a book that hurt many people. Lindy realized before
her husband did that the book would be a disaster and made
Carpenter remove some of the more memorable remarks, but
much damage was done anyway, and in after years she would
say to him 'HC' when he seemed on the point of supplying
interesting copy to other interviewers.

He had an exceptional gift for anecdote and found it very
hard to resist. He got away with it most of the time because he
had a way of making people feel worthy of his trust. This is a
trick few clergymen can work on journalists.

There may be no lasting achievements of Robert Runcie's
primacy, after an earlier life of remarkable promise and success.
He did as much to sustain the unity of the Church of England
and the Anglican Communion as any man could; and he did
more than seemed humanly possible to show why that unity
was worth preserving. He was brave, honourable, gentle, long-
suffering and wonderfully witty. Those who worked for him
loved him. He made Christian truth seem personally as well as
intellectually attractive: in that sense, he was a witness, or, in
the Greek, *martyr*.

Greatly Beloved: Robert Runcie – In Thanksgiving

RICHARD CHARTRES

An address given at the memorial service for Robert Runcie, 8 November 2000 in Westminster Abbey

The last occasion on which I heard Robert Runcie speak in public was in support of an appeal for another abbey, St Albans. There had been some muddle about who, precisely, was to speak and Robert modestly suggested that he was a mere substitute and he told a story about Archbishop Donald Coggan. Archbishop Coggan had been invited to a garden party with the promise of a strawberry and cream tea. When approaching the gate, however, in common with the other guests, he was handed a note which read: 'Owing to an unseasonable unavailability of strawberries, prunes will be served'.

That's how I feel now. Robert Runcie was himself the master of the memorial address and I suspect that only he could have done justice to such a rich life.

Typically, however, he was also modestly dubious about this occasion and wondered whether it would really be necessary. In the event, the Abbey has not been able to hold the numbers of people who have applied for tickets. The diversity of those of us who have assembled testifies to Robert Runcie's gift for friendship and the breadth of his sympathies and interests. We profess or are agnostic about many faiths. We come from many countries, from every part of the Christian Church and from the provinces of the Anglican Communion. We come not as formal representatives but drawn by a sense of personal friendship for a man who was and is greatly beloved.

I can see him in my mind's eye now, a relaxed style of delivery giving no hint of the meticulous preparation and hard work which went into his public addresses. He had a great respect for the word and had a good ear for which words were still potent and usable and which had become decrepit. He also had a penetrating intellect and could spot the flaws in arguments so readily that it made the process of composing public statements very laborious, but his gifts were perhaps most obvious in the thousands of personal letters of sympathy and encouragement which he wrote in his own hand.

This was hidden work and there was much about his deepest convictions which was also hidden. As with so many of his generation, wartime service was formative. He did not often refer to those years but the death of a comrade and the revelations at Belsen of the dark side of human nature played a large part in pushing him towards ordination as a priest. First-hand experience of the horror of the Shoah also gave him a lifelong commitment to Christian–Jewish relations. He was part of a generation of priests marked by the war who believed that the Christian community still had the potential to change the world.

In the years following he worked hard, in Gosforth, back in Cambridge and at Cuddesdon, anxious not to let people down. At the same time he also had a pronounced competitive streak which came out in his convictions for speeding on the Stevenage by-pass while he was Bishop of St Albans. He made the sports pages of the *Daily Mirror* and became the hero of the church-wardens of the diocese.

The role of Archbishop of Canterbury is very frequently frustrating. The Archbishop is mistakenly compared by the world with a managing director and blamed for every conceivable failure in the Church, but when he attempts to bring about some change and seize the levers he finds that there are no connecting rods. Archbishops lead by setting a style which can be deeply influential but often does not translate easily into a list of achievements.

This is a generation of seekers who are sceptical of ecclesiastical claims to have all the answers and who demand seriousness about the mystery and the paradoxes of life and suffering. As we have heard from Robert Runcie's enthronement sermon it was his talent and ambition to communicate with such people.

The Soul of Britain survey commissioned by the BBC records the familiar fact that the credibility of all institutions, including the churches, continues to decline. At the same time, however, the numbers of people admitting to significant personal spiritual experiences has greatly increased over the past decade. Under half the sample answering similar questions in 1989 could point to significant experiences of the spiritual realm. By 2000 this figure was over three-quarters of those questioned. One of the most frequent tributes to Robert as a bishop is that, whatever the doubts and questions of the person he was with, he was able to meet them where they were without judging them or preaching at them.

He was a very contemporary Christian leader in another respect. The Church of England had a central part in the nineteenth-century version of Our Island Story. The end of Empire, a more cosmopolitan British population and our participation in a wired up world presents a challenge to the nature of British identity and also to the identity of the Church of England. Robert made a contribution to developing a new identity in a process which has perhaps only just begun. He was a wonderful ambassador and made connections which have borne rich fruit.

The equation of Catholic and alien was a part of the old story. The way in which the Pope was received at Canterbury in 1982 was an important milestone in honouring the Roman Catholic strand in our story. Robert had first met the Pope in Africa at the start of his archiepiscopate. The encounter was to take place in Accra in Ghana. Robert briefed Cardinal Hume about what was planned by telephone. The Cardinal was enthusiastic but finally asked, 'But Robert, there's one thing I do not understand, why is it necessary to meet the Pope in a car?'

The Canterbury service was the very first time in the history of the West that the Pope had participated in the worship of a non-Roman Catholic Church and *pace* certain recent commentators John Paul II certainly behaved as if he were visiting a sister Church. Pope and Archbishop stood side by side before Augustine's chair where a book of the Gospels was enthroned – the very book sent by Pope Gregory the Great to the first Archbishop of Canterbury.

A little later, in connection with the five-hundredth anniversary of the birth of Martin Luther, Robert as Archbishop visited Germany and the work he did was a major stimulus for the Meissen Conversations and Agreement that followed.

Through a demanding programme of visits to the churches

of the Anglican Communion he encouraged Anglicans towards a new inclusive and confident identity by personal friendship and by telling the story of the connection between Canterbury and the Communion in a way that defused any suspicion of English condescension.

His stamina was remarkable. After a month in Nigeria in the hottest time of the year just before the rains, his aides, Terry Waite and the Chaplain, were exhausted but the Archbishop was still valiantly working through his programme. We reached Kano and the Archbishop of Nigeria indicated a TV camera and said to Cantuar, 'Pray for rain'. He did so. That afternoon the heavens opened and our Muslim driver said, 'You'll be remembered in Kano.'

Making new connections and embracing a more cosmopolitan identity was work which continued to the very end of Robert's earthly life. After his death the *Oxford Companion to Christian Thought* was published, edited by the distinguished Roman Catholic scholar Adrian Hastings. It contains an article by Robert Runcie on Canterbury. Typically the author admits that the city is 'a comparatively modest urban centre in Kent' but he goes on to place Canterbury in a more cosmopolitan history with mentions of previous Greek and Italian archbishops, the architecture of the French Gothic, and the French Protestant congregation which has worshipped in the crypt since the sixteenth century. In the article, as throughout his ministry, he remembers in a way that establishes a new inclusive identity and reaffirms Canterbury's place in the effort to heal the 'historic divisions of Christianity'.

He had been accused of course of being too inclusive and emollient and in a famous phrase of firmly nailing his colours to the fence. Sometimes that is the right place for colours, to give time the chance to outflank polemics. Refusal to get down into the trenches can give the community a chance to live through difficulties without being atomized.

Where a firm stand was necessary, however, the Archbishop spoke out for Christian conscience. In the Falklands service in St Paul's his note was Christian and penitent rather than triumphalist, as some desired. He was also attacked for his role in the publication of the *Faith in the City* report on deprivation in inner-city areas. What was rubbished then as 'Marxist' is now accepted wisdom but typically the report was not just a demand that the Government or someone else should do something, it was a challenge to the Church. The report led to the establishment of the Church Urban Fund which is still doing creative work in the inner cities, and it also changed lives. One priest said to me, 'It gave me a new sense of pride in being a part of the Church of England.'

St Augustine of Hippo in his pithy way described the Christian community at its best, *In certis, unitas. In dubiis, libertas. Et in omnibus caritas.* In the fundamentals of faith there must be unity. In disputable matters there must be freedom for debate. But in everything there must be love.

Robert's convictions formed and tested in struggle were deep, though hidden behind a veil of reticence. In worship these deep springs were refreshed. There were bedrock certainties which gave him the strength not merely to tolerate but encourage differences of opinion among those with whom he chose to work.

In certis unitas, in dubiis libertas – but the most lasting thing is love. Family life was not without its occasional tempests but family was the place where Robert could be entirely himself. Lindy, James and Rebecca and now a wider family were and are united in love. Robert was a man greatly beloved by a huge circle of friends.

In the last years, after Robert had laid down the burden of office, this element in his life was distilled out. Many people shrink once they have lost the trappings of status and visible power. Robert, by contrast, seemed to shake off a role that had become constricting. He became more himself. The playfulness of earlier years revived. His sympathies continued to enlarge. He made no secret of his cancer but, far from becoming self-obsessed, he found that his ability to encourage others who were locked in the same battle increased.

We believe that what has turned to love in our lives will never perish. St Paul said: 'Though our outward man perish yet the inward man is renewed day by day' (2 Corinthians 4.16). We miss him, his friendship and his humour but, in the midst of the tears, we can – in the word which rings through St Paul – rejoice.

Notes

1. Originally published in the *Independent*, 13 July 2000.

Introduction: Runcie: Gownsman and Swordsman

1. Peter Hennessy, *The Prime Minister: The Office and Its Holders since 1945*, London: Allen Lane – The Penguin Press 2000, p. 249.
2. Hennessy, *The Prime Minister*, p. 251.
3. Owen Chadwick, *Michael Ramsey: A Life*, Oxford: Clarendon Press, 1990, p. 107.
4. Personal conversation with the author.
5. Anthony Howard, 'What Is the Church to Do, for God's Sake?' *The Times*, Friday, 13 April 2000 (Good Friday).
6. James Runcie, *My Father*, Channel 4, 16 December 2000.

Prelude: Bishop, Companion and Friend: Runcie Remembered

1. Ann Lewin, 'After Word'.

1. Reluctant Crusader: Runcie and the State

1. The Report of the Archbishop of Canterbury's Commission on Urban Priority Areas, *Faith in the City*, London: Church House Publishing, 1985.
2. The Church Urban Fund was established following the debate in the General Synod on *Faith in the City*. The report proposed the establishing of the Church Urban Fund and initially dioceses were requested to raise an initial capital sum of £20 million which was to be used with matching funding to set up a great variety of initiatives in urban priority areas. The fund continues to sponsor similar work.

2. Nudging the Government: Runcie and Public Affairs

1. Adrian Hastings, *Robert Runcie*, London: Mowbray, 1991, p. 84.
2. Robert Runcie, *One Light for One World*, London: SPCK, 1988, pp. 139–46.
3. Alan Webster, letter, *The Times*, 7 May 1996.
4. John Major, *The Autobiography*, London: HarperCollins, 1999, pp. 139–46.

5. Hastings, *Robert Runcie*, p. 97.
6. The Report of the Archbishop of Canterbury's Commission on Urban Priority Areas, *Faith in the City*, London: Church House Publishing, 1985, p. 111.
7. Hastings, *Robert Runcie*, p. 95.
8. *Synodical Government in the Church of England: Being the Report of a Commission Appointed by the Archbishops of Canterbury and York*, London: Church Information Office, 1966.
9. *Canterbury Diocesan News*, January 1991.
10. Humphrey Carpenter, *Robert Runcie: The Reluctant Archbishop*, London: Hodder and Stoughton, 1996, p. 284.
11. John Krumm, *Letters from Lambeth*, Forward Movement Publications, 1988, p. 96.
12. Paul Welsby, contribution to David L. Edwards (ed.), *Robert Runcie: A Portrait by His Friends*, London: HarperCollins, 1990, p. 69.
13. G. K. A. Bell, *Randall Davidson*, Vol. 2, Oxford: Oxford University Press, 1935, p. 1161.
14. Runcie, *One Light for One World*, p. 136.
15. Quoted in Humphrey Carpenter, *Robert Runcie: The Reluctant Archbishop*, London: Hodder and Stoughton, 1996, p. 384.

3. *Facing Both Ways: Runcie's Social Vision*

1. W. S. F. Pickering, *A Social History of the Diocese of Newcastle 1882–1982*, Stocksfield: Oriel Press, 1981, pp. 70–1.
2. Denis Healey, *The Time of My Life*, London: Michael Joseph, 1989, p. 143.
3. John A. T. Robinson, 'The House Church and the Parish Church', *Theology*, Vol. LIII, No. 362, August 1950, pp. 283–9.
4. Ernest Southcott, *The Parish Comes Alive*, London: Mowbray, 1956, p. 148.
5. *The Parliamentary Debates – House of Lords*, 5th Series, Vol. 416, 14 January 1981, p. 66.
6. Robert Runcie, *Windows onto God*, London: SPCK, 1983, p. 92.
7. Adrian Hastings, *Robert Runcie*, London: Mowbray, 1991, p. 92.
8. *Homosexual Relationships: A Contribution to Discussion*, London: Church Information Office, 1979.

5. *'I'm Robert, what's your name?': Runcie and the Anglican Communion*

1. *The Truth Shall Set You Free: The Lambeth Conference 1988*, London: Church House Publishing, 1988, p. 11–24.
2. Adrian Hastings, *Robert Runcie*, London: Mowbray, 1991, pp. 138–59.

3. Robert Runcie, *Authority in Crisis? An Anglican Response*, London: SCM Press, 1988, p. 20.
4. Robert Runcie, 'Christian Authority: Enthronement Sermon', in Runcie, *Windows onto God*, London: SPCK, 1983, pp. 1–6.
5. Runcie, 'Christian Authority', p. 2.
6. Runcie, 'Christian Authority', p. 4.
7. Robert Runcie, 'Enthronement in Uganda', in Runcie, *One Light for One World*, London: SPCK, 1988, pp. 160–4.
8. Archbishop's Presidential Address, in *Mission in a Broken World: Report of ACC8, Wales 1990*, London: Church House Publishing, 1990, p. 28.
9. *The Truth Shall Set You Free*, p. 13.
10. Robert Runcie, 'In South Africa', Sermon preached at a concelebrated Eucharist, in Runcie, *One Light for One World*, pp. 182–7.
11. Robert Runcie, Sermon, in *Bonds of Affection: Proceedings of ACC6*, Anglican Consultative Council, 1984, p. 19.
12. Robert Runcie, Presidential address, in *Mission in a Broken World*, p. 31.
13. Robert Runcie, 'Mission and Evangelism', address to the Maramon Convention, in *One Light for One World*, pp. 170–4.
14. Runcie, *Authority in Crisis?*
15. Runcie, *Authority in Crisis?*, p. 48.
16. *Women and the Episcopate: The Grindrod Report*, London: ACC, 1988.
17. Runcie, *Authority in Crisis?*, p. 48.
18. Runcie, Presidential address to ACC8, in *Mission in a Broken World*, p. 32.
19. Runcie, *Authority in Crisis?*, p. 30–31.

6. *Friendship Before Theology: Runcie and the Churches*

The Bishop of Stafford originally wrote parts of this obituary for the Ecumenical Society of the Blessed Virgin Mary of which Robert Runcie was a Patron and discrete supporter. A number of essays assessing Robert Runcie's archiepiscopate from an ecumenical perspective can be found within David L. Edwards (ed.), *Robert Runcie: A Portrait by His Friends*, London: HarperCollins, 1990.

1. Lancelot Andrewes, *Opuscula*, in Ruth Ruse and Stephen Charles Neill (eds), *A History of the Ecumenical Movement 1517–1948*, London: SPCK, 1954, p. 191.
2. Andrew Brown, 'Runcie: An Obituary', *The Independent*, 13 July 2000.

7. *Pastoral Pragmatist: Runcie as Communicator*

1. *One Light for One World*, London: SPCK, 1988.
2. *The Unity We Seek*, London: Darton Longman & Todd, 1989.
3. 'Zeebrugge Ferry Disaster', in Runcie, *One Light for One World*, p. 79.
4. Humphrey Carpenter, *Robert Runcie: The Reluctant Archbishop*, London: Hodder and Stoughton, 1996.
5. 'Gallipoli Lecture: The God of Battles and the Fight for Faith', in Runcie, *The Unity We Seek*, pp. 94–109.
6. *The Spectator*, 23 May 1998.
7. Richard Harries, *The One Genius: Reading through the Year with Austin Farrer*, London: SPCK, 1987, p. ix.

9. *Remembering a Good Man*

1. Originally published in the *Independent*, 13 July 2000.

Index